# This Book is Dedicated to:

My parents, Mr. and Mrs. Charlie Lewis Sr., who poured into me love, support, and a firm foundation in God.

Ms. Sonjia Lewis, whose critical eye for editing helped me find my writing voice for the second Lenten devotional.

My siblings, Le'Ontyne, Charlene, Reta, and Charlie, for always loving, encouraging, and supporting me.

My sister, the late Wanda F. Hendrix, who I think about often. I wish I could talk to you one more time.

Kenneth C. Harris, II, the artist who captured the struggle of Jesus Christ and Simon of Cyrene as they journeyed to the cross.

Kevin Slimp (publisher at Market Square Books), Sheri Carder Hood (editor), and Ken Rochelle (post-production editor) for giving me the opportunity to bless others again through my writing.

# STRUGGLE
## TO THE CROSS

**A LENTEN STUDY FOR INDIVIDUALS AND GROUPS**

*To: Tiffany*

*Bp. Sharma D. Lewis*

*3/14/2023*

## BISHOP SHARMA D. LEWIS

Market
Square
BOOKS

# Struggle to the Cross
## *A Lenten Study for Individuals and Groups*

©2022 Bishop Sharma D. Lewis

books@marketsquarebooks.com
141 N. Martinwood, Suite 20   Knoxville, Tennessee 37923

ISBN: 978-1-950899-68-5

Printed and Bound in the United States of America
Cover Illustration & Book Design ©2022 Market Square Publishing, LLC

Editor: Sheri Carder Hood
Post-Process Editor: Ken Rochelle
Front Cover Art: Kenneth C. Harris, II

**Unless noted otherwise, Scripture quotations are from:**

### Other Scripture quotations:

# Table of Contents

# INTRODUCTION
## Journey to Transformation
### (Part 2)

Thank you for joining me as we explore together the Lectionary Year A passage of scriptures for the next six weeks. I began the process of writing *Journey to Transformation* in 2019 during my recovery from four hip surgeries. I have been humbled by the response to my writings. After prayer and discernment, I decided it was time to put the pen to paper again.

In the last three years, we have faced the COVID-19 global pandemic, January 6th insurrection, gun violence, fluctuating gas prices, and the war on Ukraine, to name a few. As you reflect during this Lenten season, I pray that you will be renewed in your faith as we journey together.

The title of the book, *Struggle to the Cross,* was birthed as I examined Jesus' last days on earth. His struggle was for us to be victorious as believers and have eternal life. My prayer is that, by reading *Struggle to the Cross,* you will see that you can conquer anything that life throws at you. John 16:33 (CEB) reminds us, "I've said these things to you so that you will have peace in me. In the world, you have distress. But be encouraged! I have conquered the world."

Lent is a season of forty days, not counting Sundays, that begins on Ash Wednesday and ends on Holy Saturday. This forty-day period of repentance and renewal preceding Easter allows us as believers of Christ to recall the Easter story and understand its meaning: that our Lord and Savior lived and died to redeem the world from sin. Because of Christ's death and resurrection, our lives *can* be renewed, as we have the power to renounce sin and begin to live for God. "Historically, Lent began as a period of fasting and preparation for Holy Baptism by converts and then became a time for penance by all Christians."[1]

Today Ash Wednesday emphasizes two themes: we confront our own mortality, and we confess our sins before God within the community. I invite you to participate in an Ash Wednesday experience. "The use of ashes as a sign of mortality and repentance has a long history in Jewish and Christian worship, and the Imposition of Ashes can be a powerful nonverbal and experiential way of participating in the call to repentance and reconciliation."[2]

As we journey together for the next six weeks, I invite you to observe Lent through introspection, repentance, forgiveness, renewal, prayer, fasting, and biblical study. Since Lent is a time for self-examination and renewal, I offer a "My Action" section each day to allow you to continue putting into practice what you have read and reflected upon daily. This will be an opportunity to experience transformation in your life and for you to be a

---

1  *The United Methodist Book of Worship,* (Nashville: The United Methodist Publishing House, 1992), p. 320.

2  Ibid, p. 321.

blessing to someone's life.

Each day's study is divided into five sections: Lenten Devotional, Selected Scriptures, Prayer, Reflection, and My Action. The scriptural quotations are from the *New International Version* unless noted otherwise. I have added a "Selected Scriptures Section" to support the daily devotions found in the *Life Application Study Bible* and the *Nelson Study Bible.*

Sundays are not counted during the Lenten season, but this study will allow you, or a group, to further engage in self-reflection. On Sundays, my personal reflection notes will ask you to reflect on the past week's study with the following questions and journaling prompt:

- Which day stood out during this week's Lenten journey?

- What did you learn about yourself and your relationship with Jesus Christ?

- Under the heading of "My Action," which day brought you great joy or difficulty? Why?

- Please journal your thoughts. (Space is available on the next page for journaling.)

## DAY ONE
# Isaiah 58:1-12

Ash Wednesday

Do you remember when you were first introduced to the discipline of fasting? Were you in the church preparing for the Lenten season? Or, did you consider fasting to lose those unwanted pounds quickly?

Fasting is an ancient biblical and spiritual tool for revitalizing the body and spirit. For centuries, people have used the spiritual discipline of fasting as a means to grow deeper into their relationship with God. The Bible illustrates many different reasons for and examples of fasting:

- Moses fasted before receiving the Ten Commandments (Deuteronomy 9:9-18).
- Elijah fasted while escaping Jezebel (1 Kings 19:4-8).
- Paul fasted after his conversion experience (Acts 9:1-9).
- Jesus fasted before being tempted by Satan and starting his public ministry (Matthew 4:1-2).

To fast biblically is going without food or drink voluntarily for a specific time and generally for religious

STRUGGLE TO THE CROSS

purposes.[3] According to scholars, the Old Testament
normally gives three common reasons for fasting: to
express distress, grief, or repentance.

Today's text, found in Isaiah 58:1-12, reveals that
abstaining from food or water was not automatically
effective in accomplishing the desires of those who fasted.
In the prophet Isaiah's time, the Israelites complained they
had fasted and God had not responded favorably.[4] Their
fasting was not acceptable to the Lord because it focused on
self-righteousness and not on justice for others.

Isaiah 58:6-7 gives clear insight into what the Lord
requires in fasting:

> *"Is this not the kind of fasting I have chosen: to
> loose the chains of injustice and untie the cords of
> the yoke, to set the oppressed free and break every
> yoke? Is it not to share your food with the hungry
> and to provide the poor wanderer with shelter—
> when you see the naked, to clothe them...?"*
>
> **Isaiah 58:6-7 (NIV)**

My mother would often say that a true measure of
your relationship with the Lord is to examine how you
treat others when they are in need. Are we committed
to loosening the bonds of wickedness, undoing the heavy
burdens, feeding the hungry, clothing the naked, and
sheltering the poor?

---

3 Youngblood, Ronald F., General Editor, *Nelson's New Illustrated Bible Dictionary*,
(Nashville: Thomas Nelson Publishers, 1995), p. 444.

4 Ibid.

## Selected Scriptures

- Zechariah 7:5
- Ezekiel 18:16-18
- Job 31:16-23

## Prayer

Lord, for the next forty days, allow me to renew my faith as I work towards a closer relationship with you. Amen.

## Reflection

How do you define justice and injustice?

Identify the injustice(s) that you have dealt with in your lifetime.

## My Action

During the Lenten season, choose one day to fast. If you are unable to fast because of a medical reason(s), please fast from a favorite pastime (for example, Facebook, Instagram, going to the movies) and use this time to meditate on Isaiah 58:1-12.

# DAY TWO

# Psalm 51

First Thursday of Lent

This well-known psalm is based on the incident recorded in 2 Samuel 11 and 12 when David committed adultery with Bathsheba and plotted to have Uriah killed in battle.

David writes this psalm confessing his sinful nature and asking God for forgiveness. According to scholars, David's confession is regarded as a model for forgiveness and true repentance in Christianity.

As a theological term, *forgiveness* refers to God's pardon for the sins of human beings.[5] *Repentance* has been described as turning away from sin, disobedience, or rebellion, and turning back to God.[6] Furthermore, repentance involves far more than intellectual change or remorse; it entails a new, or renewed, relationship with God that transforms all the dimensions of one's life, including conduct, and is akin to conversion.[7]

---

5   Ibid, p. 461.

6   Ibid, p. 1078.

7   Sakenfeld, Katharine D., General Editor, *The New Interpreter's Dictionary of the Bible, Me-R, Volume 4* (Nashville: Abingdon Press, 2009), p. 763.

When we are faced with our sinful desires that lead to a broken covenant with God, do we immediately confess and repent like David? Or, do we hope and pray that no one will find out that we are less than perfect?

On this Christian journey, I believe that how we handle our sinful desires is an indication of our spiritual maturity. The Apostle Paul reminds us in Romans 3:23 "that **all** have sinned and fall short of the glory of God." No one is exempt from the sinful nature that we are born into as humans. The beauty of our Lord and Savior is that God does not keep a track record of the sins we commit. 1 John 1:9 states, "If we confess our sins, he is faithful and just and will forgive us our sins and purify us from all unrighteousness." Confession leads us to repentance as we admit that we are sinners in need of God's grace and mercy.

Today's text opens with David expressing his intense guilt for the sin he has committed, followed by the recognition that his sinful nature alienates him from God. In verses 6-12, David appeals to God for forgiveness, cleansing of his sin, renewal of their relationship, and restoration of God's salvation. In verses 13-15, David makes a promise to serve, followed by a statement on the meaning of true worship. Finally, in verses 16-19, David pleads to God to restore the offerings of God's people. When we display our sin(s) through confession, God turns our darkness into light.

> *Those who hide their sins won't succeed, but those who confess and give them up will receive mercy.*

**Proverbs 28:3 (CEB)**

10

## Selected Scriptures

- 2 Samuel 11 and 12

- James 5:16

- Psalm 32:5

## Prayer

Lord, please forgive me for my sins. "Purify me from my sins, and I will be clean; wash me and I will be whiter than snow" (Psalm 51:7, NLT). Amen.

## Reflection

What blocks or hinders us from forgiving others and ourselves?

## My Action

Meditate on Psalm 51. Forgive yourself for any wrongdoings that you have committed and pray a prayer of repentance.

## DAY THREE
# Romans 1:8-17

First Friday of Lent

Do you feel responsible for sharing your faith with others? When was the last time you shared your faith? In this pluralistic society, do you find that by sharing your faith, you are imposing on the rights of others?

I once heard a preacher tell a story about a nonbeliever and a believer. The nonbeliever asks, "Why do you try to impose your faith on others?" The believer answers by asking the nonbeliever another question, "If you were driving on a highway one dark, rainy night and discovered that a bridge was damaged and partially washed out, would you stand with a flashlight and try to warn the oncoming traffic or would you allow a disaster?" The nonbeliever immediately answers, "I would warn the oncoming traffic." The believer responds, "I'm not trying to impose my faith onto others but trying to warn others in an effort to save them from a fatal catastrophe."

Romans 1:8-17 sets the tone of Paul's letter to the church in Rome. The passage reveals that Paul felt a deep longing to visit Rome coupled with an evangelistic obligation to preach the Gospel to mutually share and spread the faith and be fruitful. Although this may seem like unimportant information, Paul introduces the main theme of the letter: preaching the Gospel and witnessing, through our faith, the power of salvation to anyone who believes.

Paul's statement in verse 16 that he is "not ashamed of the Gospel" conveys his trust in the power of God's Word as an instrument of salvation. The Greek word for "power" is *dynamis,* from which English derives *dynamo* and *dynamite*.[8] For Paul, *dynamis* meant more than the almighty power of God revealed in nature, history, and miracles.[9] It meant God's ability and continued acts to save humanity.

Paul's statement in verse 17, "For in the gospel a righteousness from God is revealed, a righteousness that is by faith from first to last, just as it is written: 'The righteous will live by faith.'" In salvation, God seeks to replace our unrighteousness with a righteousness that God develops in us.[10] God's desire is for humanity to live, think, and act righteously. Romans 1:8-17 is a fulfillment of the Habakkuk 2:4 prophecy that the "righteous shall live by faith," foretelling the truth that Christians are saved by their faith.

---

8  Blount, Brian., General Editor, *True to Our Native Land, An African American New Testament Commentary,* (Minneapolis: Fortress Press, 2007), p. 250.

9  Ibid.

10 *Disciple's Study Bible, New International Version,* (Nashville: Holman Bible Publishers, 1998), p. 1417.

## Selected Scriptures

- Habakkuk 2:4

- Galatians 3:8

- Hebrews 11:1-6

## Prayer

Lord, please give me the eagerness and the courage to proclaim your Gospel and not be ashamed. Amen.

## Reflection

Do you truly believe in the power of the Gospel message? If so, how has it affected your life? Journal an incident where you shared the Gospel message.

## My Action

Before the Lenten season ends, share your faith with others.

# Matthew 18:1-7

First Saturday of Lent

The word *greatest* defined by vocabulary.com means the highest in quality and is synonymously described as matchless, incomparable, and outstanding. According to Dictionary.com's slang dictionary, not many people can claim to be the G.O.A.T., but those who can are the **Greatest Of All Time** in their respective fields. Most often, the acronym G.O.A.T. describes exceptional athletes like Kobe, Serena, and Simone but also musicians and other public figures.

In Mark 9:33-34, we learn that Jesus pointedly engaged in a conversation with the disciples, asking them what they had been discussing earlier. However, in the text, the disciples then question Jesus: "Who is the greatest in the kingdom of heaven?"

Jesus instructs a child to stand among them and then states, "Unless you change and become like little children, you will never enter the kingdom of heaven." I find it interesting that Jesus uses a *child t*o identify with the entrance to the kingdom. Could it be that Jesus was observing the *childish* manner of the disciples rather than a *childlike* attitude?

The disciples became so self-centered and preoccupied with the structure of Jesus' earthly kingdom that they lost sight of the divine purpose. Instead of them desiring to serve in ministry, they felt it was more important to determine their rightful positions.

It is quite easy to lose perspective on the mission of the church and compete for status and accolades. The greatest in the kingdom doesn't depend on your status, education, degrees, homes, cars, money acquired, or accomplishments.[11]

The key to being the greatest is further clarified in the scripture as Jesus states, "Whoever humbles himself like this child is the greatest in the kingdom of heaven." Unfortunately, society depicts the character of humility as suffering or weakness. However, to understand Jesus' instruction about humility, one must observe the character of a child.[12] Children are innocent, naïve, and trusting towards their parents. It is their innocence and trusting nature that enables them to be open to the presence of God. Scholars have suggested that "to become like a child" has many connotations.

Lastly, Jesus warns the disciples in Matthew 18:5-9 that there will be eternal punishment for anyone who causes harm to "these little ones." As leaders, it is our responsibility to help young people develop their faith and

---

11 Lewis, Sharma D., *Journey to Transformation,* (Knoxville: Market Square Books, 2020), p. 16.

12 Ibid.

protect them from harm that may lead to sin. Matthew 18:1-7 and Matthew 9:22-26 exemplify Jesus' tender spot for children and his passion to protect them from harm.

As writer John Ruskin says, "If you want to work for the Kingdom of God, and to bring it, and to enter into it, there is just one condition to be first accepted. You must enter into it as children, or not at all."[13]

## Selected Scriptures

- Matthew 19:14

- 1 Peter 2:2

- Luke 17:1-2

## Prayer

Lord, help me to possess a *child-like* faith to enter the kingdom of heaven. Amen.

---

13 Richards, Lawrence O., *Devotional Commentary,* (Colorado Springs: Cook Communications Ministries, 2002), p. 668.

19

## Reflection

How do you define *greatest* in a spiritual context?

How do we equip our young children to learn about the faith?

## My Action

During this Lenten season, take an opportunity to learn about and improve child safety in the church.

# First Sunday in Lent

## My Personal Reflection Notes

*Reflect on this past week.*

What day stood out during this week's Lenten journey?

What did you learn about yourself and your relationship with Jesus Christ?

Which "My Action" of the week brought you great joy or difficulty? Why?

Please journal your thoughts.

## DAY FIVE
# I Kings 19:1-8

*First Monday of Lent*

Have you ever felt depressed? Do you presently suffer from depression? December 12, 2021, was the hardest day of my adult life, and I dreaded the day as it approached. I remember people telling me that the "first" year was the hardest. I must concur they were right. The "first" birthday, Thanksgiving, and Christmas were very difficult.

I remember waking up, reaching for my phone, and posting pictures of my mother on my Facebook page. I wanted to celebrate her life, but I couldn't find the strength to get out of bed. Therefore, I laid there and reflected on my beautiful mother, who gave birth to me on November 13. I remembered how she taught me to love the beauty of my brown skin. She would often say, "You don't need makeup—let your outward beauty show." I reflected on how she lived to be ninety years young.

My mother was not afraid to get on a plane and travel around the country. One of my fondest memories was when she stood with me on July 16, 2016, with tears of joy when I accepted my election as the first Black woman elected to the Episcopacy in the Southeastern Jurisdiction of The

United Methodist Church.

On that December day, I found myself crying as if her passing had just happened, and I decided that I didn't want to be bothered by anyone that day. I buried myself in my tears and drifted back to sleep. I awakened to see that family, friends, and colleagues had called. Many people posted kind condolences and prayers on my Facebook page.

However, after hours of sleeping, I realized I was hungry and needed to get out of bed. I ate and went for a long walk, hoping that walking would take my mind off my sadness. Yes, this was the first anniversary of my mother's death.

I realized I was depressed. Depressed! No one likes to admit they are depressed. No one likes to admit they suffer from clinical depression or mental illness, but in today's society, it is a common struggle! The now-prevalent medications of Paxil and Zoloft were almost unheard of ten years ago. Now you cannot watch television without seeing a commercial advertising medications to treat depression or mental illness.

According to Mayo Clinic clinical psychologist Dr. Craig Sawchuk, "Depression is a mood disorder that causes a persistent feeling of sadness and loss of interest. Also called a major depressive disorder or clinical depression, it affects how you feel, think, and behave and can lead to a variety of emotional and physical problems."[14]

I never thought I was depressed; but in hindsight, I felt the symptoms that day. When depression strikes, what do you do? Do you ignore it or seek medical/spiritual advice?

---

14 www.mayoclinic.org/diseases-conditions/depression/symptoms-causes/syc-20356007.

Is it a mark of our spiritual weakness? Does depression indicate a lack of faith?

As we examine the text, we see that Elijah is feeling a deep sense of depression after the victory on Mount Carmel. As we read, we witness how God treats God's prophet's depression and gives us insights on how to help ourselves. The text opens with the threat from Jezebel to end Elijah's life. Elijah flees and finds himself discouraged, alone with desires to end his life (1 Kings 19:4). It is in verses 5-8 that God ministers to the physical needs of Elijah by providing food and water to sustain him to travel to Mount Horeb.

It is quite easy to feel lost and despondent when depression strikes. In times of great turmoil, we must remember that God is a loving and compassionate God who heals the broken. Depression is a struggle for many, and we must never feel ashamed or alone. God gives us the spiritual tools of prayer, fasting, and worship to conquer the low feelings we experience in life. God also gives us the wisdom to seek wise counsel when we are constantly battling with our emotions.

## Selected Scriptures

- I Kings 18

- Deuteronomy 31:8

- Psalm 34:17-18

## Prayer

"Heal me, Lord, and I will be healed; save me and I will be saved, for you are the one I praise" (Jeremiah 17:14). Please guard my heart against depression and help me fight against the challenges I face today.

## Reflection

Why is there a societal stigma about the disease of depression and mental illness? How do we educate our churches/communities?

When you are feeling depressed, how do you handle it?

## My Action

If you are feeling depressed or suffer from depression, please seek the wisdom of a medical/spiritual professional.

# Genesis 4:1-16

First Tuesday of Lent

Genesis 4:1-16 is a story that most people are familiar with from the Bible. The phrase in verse 9, "Am I my brother's keeper?" is also readily known. The text opens with the birth of Cain and Abel, followed by the description of both brothers. Cain, the firstborn, is a farmer, and Abel, the younger brother, is a shepherd. The brothers offer the fruits of their labor as a sacrifice to God. Unfortunately, God only favors the offering of Abel. As a result, Cain is angry, feels rejected, and invites Abel to the field. While they are in the field, Cain murders his brother. The Lord says to Cain, "Where is your brother Abel?" "I don't know," he replies. "Am I my brother's keeper?"

The relationship dynamics between Cain and Abel have been used in many works of art, plays, novels, and DC Comics featured in TV series and on the big screen.

What are we to learn from the first children created by Adam and Eve? We learn that our actions, attitudes, and the consequences of sin have devastating repercussions. According to scholars, Abel, the first murder victim, is sometimes perceived as the first martyr while Cain, the first murderer, is sometimes perceived as an ancestor of evil, violence, and greed. God cautions Cain in verse 7 about the struggle of sin: "If you do what is right, will you not be accepted? But if you do not do what is right, sin is crouching at your door; it desires to have you, but you must rule over it."

The sin that manifests in our lives will take us further than we anticipate going. Cain's petty jealousy and his insincere offering to God led him to kill his brother, to be barred from his home, and condemned by God to a life of wandering until his death.

Finally, this story reveals that God's grace and mercy are always available to God's children. God gives Cain a second chance by allowing him a new life in a different place. God places a mark on him to prevent him from being killed by others.

## Selected Scriptures

- Hebrews 11:4

- I John 3:12

- Psalm 51:11

## Prayer

Lord, I am my brothers' and sisters' guardian. "And what does the Lord require of me? To act justly and to love mercy and to walk humbly with my God" (Micah 6:8). Amen.

## Reflection

Why did God reject Cain's offering and accept Abel's offering?

Why did Cain murder Abel? How does jealousy affect the quality of our relationships?

## My Action

If you have any ought against a brother or sister, please attempt to reconcile and mend any wrongdoings.

# Psalm 32

First Wednesday of Lent

Psalm 32 is one of the seven penitential psalms stressing repentance and forgiveness of sins. In this psalm, David expresses his joy that God has forgiven him for committing sins against Bathsheba and Uriah.

According to *Nelson's Bible Dictionary*, "Forgiveness is characterized as God's pardon of the sins of human beings." As believers, we must continue to practice forgiveness because we know that forgiveness is directly linked to Jesus Christ. His sacrificial death on the cross and his resurrection prove this point.

God's forgiveness demands that we forgive others because grace brings responsibility and obligation. God wants to forgive sinners because forgiveness has always been a part of God's loving character. As Christians, we are required to forgive those who sin against us.

How many times in our lives do we need to forgive others? How often do we stand in need of forgiveness?

According to Matthew 18:21-22:

*Then Peter came to Jesus and asked, "Lord, how many times shall I forgive my brother or sister who sins against me? Up to seven times?" Jesus answered, "I tell you, not seven times, but seventy-seven times."*

Forgiveness brings about an intentional decision to change how we feel about what happened. Archbishop Desmond Tutu captures how vital forgiveness is for human relations with his memoir's title, *There is No Future Without Forgiveness.*

As we examine the text, Psalm 32:1-2 reveals several facets of God's forgiveness:

• Transgressions are forgiven.

• Sins are covered.

• God doesn't count our sins against us.

In these verses, David shares that forgiveness brings true joy. In verses 3-5, David shares how unconfessed sin robbed him of his relationship with God. Unconfessed sin harms our spiritual souls, and forgiveness restores our relationship with God (verses 6-7). David noted that the restored fellowship makes divine guidance possible again (verses 8-10). Finally, the psalmist, David, is able to rejoice in the Lord (verse 11).

## Selected Scriptures

- Psalm 38

- Psalm 51

- Psalm 102

## Prayer

O Lord, my sins are forever before me. I confess my faults and ask for your forgiveness. Restore me, O Lord, to be in fellowship with you. Amen.

## Reflection

Why is it difficult for us to acknowledge and confess our sin(s) before God?

What happens when we have unconfessed sin(s) in our lives?

## My Action

Meditate on Psalm 130 (penitential psalm). Confess your sin(s) before God and ask God for forgiveness.

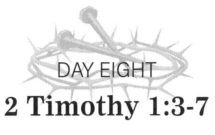

# 2 Timothy 1:3-7

Second Thursday of Lent

The scripture passage of 2 Timothy 1:3-7 sets a tone encouraging Timothy to remain faithful to the Gospel and to exercise bold leadership. In verse 6, Paul reminds Timothy "to stir up the gift of God which is in you through the laying on of my hands" (NKJV). The Apostle Paul writes his farewell letter to Timothy and the church while he is awaiting execution in a Roman prison. Timothy—who is now the pastor of the church in Ephesus—once on fire for God, has allowed his fire to go out. Paul urges his beloved son to rekindle his spiritual gift so that his gift becomes effective again.

Paul's message remains relevant for the church now as we continue to recover from the COVID-19 pandemic. The pandemic has impacted how we view the church; therefore, how we minister is different. I feel that the preventative medicine for stagnation in the body of Christ is revealed in the words spoken to Timothy: it's time for the body of Christ "to stir up the gifts of God."

According to *Webster's Dictionary*, to "stir" means:

**a) to agitate things a bit; b) to disturb; and c) to disrupt.**

What things are you agitating, disturbing, or disrupting in the Kingdom of God? Are you using the spiritual gift(s) that is in you? Is your passion for mission and ministry still energizing your soul?

I believe there are three ways to "stir up the gift" within you. First, you must recognize that you have a gift. The Bible teaches that all believers are blessed with at least one gift. 1 Corinthians 12:7 states, "Now to each one the manifestation of the Spirit is given for the common good."

Spiritual gifts are extraordinary abilities that the Holy Spirit gives to a believer to build up the body of Christ. Nonbelievers are not spiritually gifted. Various gifts are distributed to bring diversity to the unified body of Christ. I once heard that the desire to discover, develop, and deploy our spiritual gift(s) should be like a fire blazing within us.

Secondly, you must make a conscious effort to utilize your gift for the common good of the body of Christ. What good is it for you to have the gift of evangelism if you don't share the Gospel message? The purpose of our spiritual gifts is to edify, encourage, and strengthen the church. In 1 Corinthians 12:31, Paul encourages Christians to "eagerly desire the greater gifts." We should pray and ask God to show us how to use our spiritual gifts for the body of Christ.

Finally, to rekindle the spiritual gift, we need a fresh filling of the Holy Spirit. I believe the body of Christ needs a fresh wind and a fresh fire of the Holy Spirit to blow over our dead souls as demonstrated in Acts 2:1-4. The Holy

Spirit, a member of the Godhead, bears witness to God the Father and God the Son. The Holy Spirit is the source of personal testimony and revelation. Also known as the Comforter, the Holy Spirit can calm our fears and give us hope for the future.

## Selected Scriptures

- Acts 2:1-13

- I Corinthians 12:1-31

- I Timothy 4:14

## Prayer

O Lord, please breathe on me right now a fresh anointing of the Holy Spirit. Amen.

## Reflection

What are your top three spiritual gifts?

How do you utilize your spiritual gifts for the Kingdom of God?

## My Action

If you do not know your spiritual gifts, please take a spiritual gift inventory at www.spiritualgiftstest.com. If you do know your spiritual gifts, please take a refresher spiritual gifts Bible study course.

# Psalm 121

### Second Friday of Lent

There was a song recorded by the Brooklyn Tabernacle Choir, which is very applicable to the text for today. Please take a few minutes and listen to "My Help Cometh from the Lord." The refrain:

> *Upon thy right hand, upon thy right hand*
>
> *No, the sun shall not smite thee (no, the sun shall not smite me by day)*
>
> *Nor the moon by night,*
>
> *He shall preserve thy soul even forever more (even forever more)*
>
> *My help (my help) my help (comes from you, Lord Jesus) my help (all of help) all of help cometh from the Lord...*[15]

On March 8, 2020, I returned from the Holy Land with clergy and laity from the Virginia Annual Conference. The world was hit with the dreaded disease called COVID-19,

---

15 Brooklyn Tabernacle Choir, "My Help Cometh from the Lord," 1999.

also commonly known as "the pandemic." The world assumed that this disease would only last a few months. No one suspected that people would lose their lives in record numbers, people would die alone, and the entire world would be in need of help. Help came in many forms: daily instructions from Dr. Anthony Fauci, the Center for Disease Control, our community advocacy, and the church community.

As an Episcopal leader, I found myself seeking help from many resources with the intent of keeping everyone safe and informed in the annual conference.

However, one day as I was reflecting and studying, I ran across a song released in 1999 by the famous Brooklyn Tabernacle Choir that ministered to my spirit. Amid the chaotic, unprecedented circumstances and a shutdown world, this song reminded me that our "help" comes from the Lord.

In today's text, the psalmist gives us the promise that the Lord is our helper. I pray that you will have the assurance in knowing that there is no problem that God can't solve. We must come to understand that our Lord and Savior is bigger than any problem. I'm a living witness as I've recovered from four hip surgeries, led the annual conference through disaffiliations from The United Methodist Church, and endured racism. I know emphatically that God is my helper!

Psalm 121 is classified as one of the "psalms of ascents." The psalms of ascents (Psalms 120-134) constitute a series of pilgrimage songs that stress trust in God and regard the temple as the locus of worship and blessings.[16]

As we examine the text, there is an affirmation in Psalm 121:1-2 that our help is from the Lord. Psalm 124:8 states, "Our help is in the name of the Lord, the Maker of heaven and earth." These two psalms of ascents reassure the reader that God is the creator and helper.

The text also leads us to a word of praise to our God who does not slumber but watches over God's children (Psalm 121:3-6). Scholars record that, on pilgrimages to Jerusalem, the people would often stop and sleep for replenishment. There is an assurance from the psalmist that God protects God's people.

As I listened to the Brooklyn Tabernacle Choir sing "My Help Cometh from the Lord," I felt assured that, no matter what I was facing during the pandemic, my God would see me through.

Finally, the psalmist reveals in Psalm 121:7-8 that God will protect God's people from daily harm.

## Selected Scriptures

- Psalm 91

- Isaiah 41:10

- Psalm 46:1-2

---

16 Sakenfeld, Katharine D., General Editor, *The New Interpreter's Dictionary of the Bible, Me-R, Volume 4,* (Nashville: Abingdon Press, 2009), p. 677.

## Prayer

O Lord, your Word in Hebrews 13:6 reminds me, "The Lord is my helper; I will not fear; what can man do to me?" Amen.

## Reflection

During the pandemic, how did you or your church help the community at large?

Describe an incident in your life where the Lord has been a protector.

## My Action

Pick an organization or ministry in your church and volunteer during the Lenten season.

## DAY TEN
# Luke 7:1-10

*Second Saturday of Lent*

My therapist always tells me to give my feelings "words." I always find this exercise very life-giving, specifically in how I'm feeling in the moment. My mother cautioned us as kids to "be careful what you say to one another." She always reminded us that words can hurt, and, once said, they can't be taken back.

I remember the kids in my neighborhood would often say, "Sticks and stones may break my bones, but words will never hurt me," a childhood rhyme often used as a defense against name-calling or bullying. I was taught as a child that words can build up your esteem and tear it down in a matter of seconds.

James 3:9-10 reminds us, "With the tongue we praise our Lord and Father, and with it we curse human beings, who have been made in God's likeness. Out of the same mouth come praise and cursing." Proverbs 18:21 confirms this by saying, "The tongue has the power of life and death." The Bible teaches us that our tongues have a lot of power. Used appropriately, words can warrant a positive outcome; but misused, they can destroy and warrant repercussions.

In our meditation, we witness a conversation where Jesus, for the first time, extends his ministry of healing to a Gentile household. Jesus is quite impressed by the "great faith" of the Gentile officer, and he restores the health to the Gentile's critically ill servant by simply speaking a "word" from a distance. The power of Jesus' word is confirmed when the Gentile returns to the house and discovers the servant healed.

## Selected Scriptures

- Proverbs 13:3

- Ephesians 4:29

- Romans 4:17

## Prayer

O Lord, give me a tame tongue. Let me think before I speak. Let me build others up and not tear them down. Amen.

## Reflection

How do we tame our tongue?

How do we use words to edify the body of Christ?

## My Action

Reflect or share a moment where "words" were spoken in your life to build you up or tear you down. How did you feel?

# Second Sunday in Lent

## My Personal Reflection Notes

*Reflect on this past week.*

What day stood out during this week's Lenten journey?

What did you learn about yourself and your relationship with Jesus Christ?

Which "My Action" of the week brought you great joy or difficulty? Why?

Please journal your thoughts.

# Numbers 21:4-9

Second Monday of Lent

Numbers 20 and 21 contain a loose collection of stories that provide a transition from the wandering and death in the wilderness to holy war in the Transjordan.[17] Scholars conclude that the long journey around the land of Edom was crucial because the King of Edom refused to grant Moses' request for passage through his territory (Numbers 20:14-21). The long journey causes the Israelites to grow impatient. Therefore, they complain again to Moses and God about the lack of bread and water and about the quality of the food, which they detested.

In Numbers 21:4-9, God's anger manifests itself when God sends venomous snakes among the Israelites. After many people are bitten and die from snakebites, the Israelites confess their sin to Moses, and then Moses intercedes on their behalf.

Throughout the Old Testament, we are all too familiar with the constant grumbling of the Israelites and God's compassion shown for God's people. Psalm 78, a wisdom

---

17 Gaventa, Beverly Roberts and David Petersen, Editors, *The New Interpreter's Bible, One Volume Commentary,* (Nashville: Abingdon Press, 2010), p. 96.

49

psalm written by Asaph, reveals God's kindness to a rebellious Israelite people. In Psalm 78, we learn the sources of Israel's complaints:

- Their spirits were not faithful to God (78:2).
- They refused to obey God's law (78:10).
- They forgot the miracles God had performed for them (78:11).

The focus of the story is not the deadly bite of the venomous snakes but their healing power. Once the Israelites confess their sins before God, God instructs Moses to "make a snake and put it up on a pole; anyone who is bitten can look at it and live." Moses makes a replica of the snake called *Nahash Nehoshet*, the serpent of bronze," which has the power to heal anyone who looks at it.[18]

This story relates to the incident reported in 2 Kings 18:4 where King Hezekiah destroys the bronze serpent because of its association with pagan worship. The theme of divine healing is important because God keeps God's promise in Exodus 15:22-26 to be a healer for the Israelites.

Scholars believe that John 3:14-15 parallels the incident in Numbers 21:4-9. As Moses' act saved the people from death by serpent bite, so Jesus' crucifixion saves his people from death and opens the door to eternal life.[19]

---

18 Ibid, p. 97.

19 Mays, James L., General Editor, *Harper Collins Bible Commentary,* (San Francisco: Harper Collins, 2000), p. 963.

## Selected Scriptures

- John 3:14-15

- Psalm 78

- Numbers 20:4-5

## Prayer

O Lord, how excellent is your name upon the earth! I pray that the lost will come to know you and have the opportunity to make you their Lord.

## Reflection

Have you confessed Jesus Christ as your personal Lord and Savior? If so, when and where? Describe your experience. If not, please pray the prayer below:

*Dear God, I know I'm a sinner, and I ask for your forgiveness. I believe Jesus Christ is your Son. I believe that he died for my sin and that you raised him to life. I want to trust him as my Savior and follow him as Lord from this day forward. Guide my life and help me to do your will. I pray this in the name of Jesus. Amen.*[20]

---

20 Billy Graham Evangelistic Association, PeaceWithGod.net, accessed August 12, 2019.

Please locate a church to continue to strengthen your faith as you have prayed the prayer of salvation.

## My Action

Download from YouTube and listen to the hymn "Lift High the Cross."

## DAY TWELVE
# Isaiah 65:17-25

Second Tuesday of Lent

In the last three years, death and dying have taken on a new dimension of meaning for me. During the pandemic, many people were forced to die alone with only acquaintances and medical professionals they met in the hospital. Funeral homes, cemeteries, and crematoria had to adopt new approaches to mortuary science to accommodate the unpredictable deaths. The church community had to enforce new policies to keep people safe while still maintaining a level of respect for grieving families. It was difficult for pastors to keep up with the changing church protocols and even harder to provide pastoral care. Even though we are approaching year three of the pandemic, the care and concern for death and dying have become a crucial matter.

One of the hardest areas of church life is providing respectful pastoral care during the illness of a church member that leads to death. I have always felt a sense of urgency to make sure the family is especially comforted during this time. In doing so, I have experienced and witnessed many sacred moments during a family time of bereavement.

As I began my ministerial career, my district superintendent (ministerial supervisor) told me, "Pastoral care will not necessarily grow a church, but the lack of pastoral care will kill a church." These words of wisdom resonate in my ears every time we host a funeral. We always strive to provide excellent pastoral care, which includes addressing the needs of the deceased's family, helping with the viewing and visitations, communicating with others, and guiding the family through the order of service. I firmly believe that providing excellent pastoral care and worshipping God during this fragile time is paramount in helping families to grieve.

There are many resources families can use to bring healing during times of grief: a favorite poem, a pictorial montage, scriptural passages, singing, and reflection on the deceased's life.

I have found that the passage of scripture for today's reflection brings great strength and comfort to families as they worship God during this vulnerable time.

Isaiah 65:17-18 states:

> *See, I will create new heavens and a new earth.*
> *The former things will not be remembered, nor*
> *will they come to mind. But be glad and rejoice*
> *forever in what I will create, for I will create*
> *Jerusalem to be a delight and its people a joy.*

The prophet Isaiah has described the pictorial image of the new heavens and the new earth. The creation of a new heaven and earth refers to God as the one who "creates" new things, past and present.[21] What would this new heaven and new earth look like?

I read this text through the lens of John in Revelation 21:4: "He will wipe every tear from their eyes. There will be no more death or mourning or crying or pain, for the old order of things has passed away." Both scriptures in Isaiah and Revelation bring comfort because the pictorial description shows that God lives in eternal rest with the redeemed.

## Selected Scriptures

- 2 Peter 3:13

- Isaiah 43:18

- Isaiah 66:22-23

## Prayer

O Lord, as I reflect on the past three years, let me take strength in knowing that you have prepared a place for the redeemed.

---

21 Mays, James L., General Editor, *Harper Collins Bible Commentary,* (San Francisco: Harper Collins, 2000), p. 536.

## Reflection

How would you describe heaven?

What scriptures bring you comfort during times of grief? Why?

## My Action

Take the time to write a prayer of encouragement regarding the death of a loved one.

# DAY THIRTEEN
# Psalm 128

Second Wednesday of Lent

Psalm 128 is also classified as a "song of ascents." These wisdom psalms were sung as the Israelites traveled to Jerusalem, usually for one of the three yearly feasts. This psalm, similar to Psalm 127, depicts God's work in and through the family. The psalmist writes that a good family life must have God as the foundation. The values outlined in the meditation for today include obedience, service, respect, prosperity, and peace.

I was blessed to be the fifth of six children born to Charlie and Alethia Lewis in Statesboro, Georgia. You may recognize the name Statesboro because the Allman Brothers Band recorded the famous song "The Statesboro Blues." As a typical Southern family, we attended Sunday school and church every Sunday. I don't ever remember missing a Sunday. Rain, sleet, snow, or sunshine, we were present. My mother was the head usher, and my dad was the chair of the trustees. Every Saturday night, my mother made sure we completed our Sunday school lesson for the next day.

My parents raised us to love and take care of each other.

Most importantly, they raised us to love and be obedient to God. My mother constantly reminded us that the way to succeed in life was to work hard and be obedient to God's Word. She would often say that "biblical obedience means to hear, trust, submit, and surrender to God and God's Word." I've come to understand that my mother was not wrong. Living in obedience is a way to show your love and respect for God.

Psalm 128:1 states, "Blessed are all who fear the Lord, who walk in obedience to Him." Mom explained to us that "fear" in this passage of scripture doesn't mean to be afraid of God but to love, respect, and revere God."

For my family, living in obedience meant knowing and following God's Word. Mom often reminded us that "the way to follow and know God's Word is to read God's Word." At an early age, I found myself reading the Word and loving the Bible stories.

The best storyteller in my church was Mrs. Amanda Smith, who let me assist her on Sundays and during Vacation Bible School. Mrs. Smith was a frail, small, grey-headed woman who taught us that obedience was key to living a fruitful life. She often commented that "obedience is a way to draw near to God." As believers, why should we obey God?

First, obedience demonstrates our faith and trust in God. Faith enables us as believers to please God. *The Message* Bible reveals, "This faith is the firm foundation under everything that makes life worth living. It's our handle on what we can't see" (Hebrews 11:1). Trust is a conscious dependence on God and is found in our belief that God will indeed work on our behalf to bring God's perfect will for our lives. Proverbs 3:5-6 reveals, "Trust in the Lord with all your heart and lean not on your own understanding; in all your ways submit to him, and he will make your paths straight."

Secondly, living in obedience means following God's Word. John 14:15 reminds us that Jesus said to his disciples, "If you love me, keep my commandments." God has expectations for God's children. God is not calling us to be perfect but to be obedient to God's Word.

Thirdly, obedience is the key to receiving God's promises. There are six thousand promises of God in the Bible. God knows what is best for us. Isaiah 55:8 states:

> *For my thoughts are not your thoughts, neither are your ways my ways," declares the Lord. "As the heavens are higher than the earth, so are my ways higher than your ways and my thoughts than your thoughts."*

## Selected Scriptures

- Psalm 127

- Psalm 119:1-3

- I John 5:2-3

STRUGGLE TO THE CROSS

## Prayer

O Lord, I know that one of the ways to worship and glorify you is through my obedience. Teach me how to walk in your obedience. Amen.

## Reflection

Why is being obedient to God important? How do you show obedience to God?

What does God promise if we obey God? What personal promise(s) has God given you?

## My Action

Plan a trip with your family during this Lenten season. Carve out time to pray, reflect, and have fun with each other.

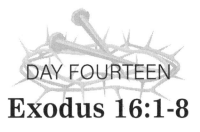

# Exodus 16:1-8

Third Thursday of Lent

I heard a story about a husband and wife who were discussing a trip to the Holy Land. Amid their research and planning, the husband uttered, "Wouldn't it be fantastic to go to the Holy Land and stand and shout the Ten Commandments from Mountain Sinai?" The wife commented sarcastically, "NO! It would be better if we stayed at home and obeyed the Ten Commandments."

Interestingly, we live in a society where the words *obey* and *obedience* have little or no meaning. No one likes to follow rules or directions anymore. Unfortunately, we witnessed this during the pandemic when people egregiously protested wearing masks to remain safe.

Our reading for today provides yet another example of God testing the obedience of the Israelites. Rick Warren, the author of the most read book in 2002, *The Purpose Driven Church*, states that God views life as a test, a trust, and a temporary assignment.[22] He goes on to state that God is continuously testing our character, faith,

---

22 Warren, Rick, *The Purpose Driven Church,* (Grand Rapids: Zondervan, 2002), p. 42.

obedience, love, integrity, and loyalty.[23]

As our story unfolds, the Israelites have left Egypt and are on their way through the Desert of Sin, a stony, barren land. As the Israelites encounter danger, scarcity of food, and inconveniences, they complain and grumble to Moses and Aaron once again.

The Israelites murmur, "If only we had died by the Lord's hand in Egypt. There we sat around pots of meats and ate all the food we wanted, but you have brought us out into this desert to starve this entire assembly to death." They complain bitterly and want to return to Egypt. Then the Lord instructs Moses that bread will be provided each day, and the Israelites will be able to gather enough for that day. The story's first lesson illustrates that God provided for the needs of the Israelites.

I can't remember a time in my upbringing—or in my life at all—when God didn't provide for me and my family's needs. My mother and grandmother always said, "God may not come when you want him, but he is always right on time." As a young child, this statement didn't mean much to me, but as I have grown older, I can testify that God has been my *Jehovah-Jireh*, God who provides.

I love Tamela Mann's song entitled "God Provides," specifically the first two stanzas, which beautifully anchor me in my faith:

> **God provides, so why do I worry about my life**
> **When you come to my rescue a thousand times**
> **Every other voice it is a lie**
> **God provides.**

23 Ibid, p. 42.

*In ways I can't explain and can't deny*
*The little that I have He multiplies*
*Just when I feel He won't show up on time*
*God provides.*[24]

In Exodus 16:5, God instructs Moses that, on the sixth day, the Israelites are to prepare what they bring in and that the amount provided will be twice as much as they gathered on the other days. The story's second lesson reveals that God wanted to test their obedience to see if they would obey God's detailed instructions.

Upon examination of the scriptures, I believe obedience comes with rewards, and disobedience yields consequences. The question that faces us daily is whom do we obey? As believers, we must approach every moment in time with God's voice and be obedient to God's plan. God's plan and purpose for your life are not dependent upon what you can or can't do. It depends on your willingness to do what God instructs you to do.

Finally, Moses and Aaron say to all the Israelites, "You will know that it was the Lord when he gives you meat to eat in the evening and all the bread you want in the morning"—despite your grumbling. Interestingly, after God's deliverance from the hands of the Egyptians and the provisions of water in the Desert of Shur, couldn't they see that supplying food was nothing for their God?

---

24 Mann, Tamela, "God Provides Lyrics," June 2016. © Kobalt Music Publishing Ltd., Songwriter, Kirk Franklin.

## Selected Scriptures

- Numbers 33:11-12

- I Corinthian 10:10

- Isaiah 58:11

## Prayer

O Lord, help me to know that you have a proven track record. Amen.

## Reflection

Reflect on how God has tested your obedience. What was the outcome? What did you learn about yourself as you were going through your test?

## My Action

Download and listen to Tamela Mann's song "God Provides."

DAY FIFTEEN

# Psalm 95

Third Friday of Lent

As a child, I loved to attend church, but, more importantly, I loved to participate in worship. I grew up in The United Methodist Church, but most of my family were Baptist or Pentecostal by family origin. I was always mesmerized by the worship services when we visited my "Pentecostal" aunts or next-door neighbors. Their choirs and musicians were always loud, vibrant, and energetic. They danced, anointed with oil, and sometimes I thought I heard an unknown tongue being spoken. The only thing that I dreaded was when the preachers caught the Holy Spirit, they didn't know when to stop preaching. Friday night revivals tended to go extra long because there was no school on Saturday. However, my parents still expected us to get up early on Saturday mornings to do our chores.

I vividly remember attending and participating in the community choir competitions in the spring. There was nothing to do in Statesboro on the weekends, so choir competitions became the new hangout. These competitions displayed the best singing and choreographic choirs. With matching robes and tambourines, the choirs processed into e sanctuary singing the most popular song playing on the radio.

I grew up listening and singing to all types of Christian music. However, my favorite groups were Kirk Franklin and the Family, John P. Kee and New Life, and Fred Hammond & Radical for Christ. I learned at an early age the importance of praising and worshipping God, and I found myself yearning to be in God's presence.

When I attended seminary, I was blessed to study under Dr. Melva Costen, Professor Emeritus of Worship at the Interdenominational Theological Center (ITC) in Atlanta, Georgia. She taught me that Christian worship is an acknowledgment of and response to the presence and power of God as revealed in Jesus the Christ through the work of the Holy Spirit. She further emphasized that worship is the celebration of all that God has done, is doing, and will do. Descriptive words associated with the understanding of worship include *praise, adoration, thanksgiving, reverence, gratitude,* and *submission. Worship* in Latin is translated as "worth-ship" or "worthiness." It is a feeling or expression of reverence and adoration for God, and its purpose is to honor and exalt our Lord and Savior. John 4:24 reminds us as believers that "God is Spirit and his worshipers must worship in the Spirit and in truth."

Psalm 95 serves as the introduction to a grouping of psalms (95-99) devoted to the theme of worship and praise. Psalm 95:3 is regarded as a royal psalm because it acknowledges God as "the great King." This psalm helps the believer to reestablish their thinking and practice concerning the importance of worship. Its three distinct movements reflect the "moods" of the worshipping community:

- Psalm 95:1-5 – the worship of God in a mood of celebration.
- Psalm 95:6-7 – the worship of God in a mood of contemplation.
- Psalm 95:8-11 – the worship of God in a mood of obedience.

Worshipping is giving of our entire self—our thoughts and our emotions—for God to use. However, what we call "worship" is too often entertainment, and we evaluate the effectiveness of worship by how *we* feel. Worship is never about us. When we come to God in worship, we should proclaim that God is worthy and worthy to be praised!

## Selected Scriptures

- Psalm 81
- Psalm 95
- Psalm 96

## Prayer

O Lord, come let us worship you in Spirit and in truth. Amen.

## Reflection

Why is it important to worship God? What are the elements of a good worship experience?

Recall the first encounter you truly felt you worshiped God. What happened? What did you feel? What songs were the musicians playing?

## My Action

Attend a worship service of another denomination or a nondenominational church.

## DAY SIXTEEN
# John 4:1-6

Third Saturday of Lent

Do you remember who nurtured and led you to salvation? How old were you? Was it a devoted member in the church or a random meeting?

In the text for today, Jesus encounters the Samaritan woman near the city of Sychar around noon. The shortest route from Judea to Galilee was through Samaria. However, Jews often avoided Samaria by traveling along the Jordan River. The tension between the Jews and Samaritans dated back to the days of the Exile. The Jews detested the Samaritans and considered them no longer "pure" Jews. The Samaritan woman was considered an outcast in the Jewish social system, and a Jewish rabbi was never allowed to talk with a woman without her husband present.

However, the exchange between Jesus and the Samaritan woman is a deep, personal, and theological conversation that eventually bears witness to his identity as the Messiah. Although culture dictated that she was inferior because of her ethnicity, sex, and marital status, none of this mattered to Jesus because he saw her in need of salvation.

When Jesus initiates the conversation at Jacob's well with a request for water, the Samaritan woman immediately puts up the ethnic barrier between them: "You are a Jew and I am a Samaritan woman. How can you ask me for a drink?" (For Jews do not associate with Samaritans.) The narrator's parenthetical aside that "Jews do not share things in common with Samaritans" understates a more deep-seated and volatile ethnic-religious rift.[25]

How many times have we experienced ethnic or religious barriers in our lifetime? Did we continue with the conversation, or did we change our trajectory? As the story unfolds, Jesus is determined to lead her to salvation, and no ethnic-religious barrier is too extreme for the Gospel message to cross. Jesus offers her salvation, and with a receptive heart, she receives it and then runs to tell others.

---

25 Sakenfeld, Katharine D., *The New Interpreter's Dictionary of the Bible,* S-Z Volume 5, (Nashville: Abingdon Press, 2009), p. 74.

## Selected Scriptures

- John 3:22, 26

- John 7:37-39

- Romans 6:23

## Prayer

O Lord, give me the heart to care and share my faith with others. Amen.

## Reflection

In your circle of influence, who is your "Samaritan" man, woman, or child?

When was the last time you led someone to salvation? Describe what happened. Did you follow up with your newly converted brother or sister in Christ?

## My Action

Share your salvation story and lead someone to Christ before the Lenten season ends.

# Third Sunday in Lent

## My Personal Reflection Notes

*Reflect on this past week.*

What day stood out to you during this week's Lenten journey?

What did you learn about yourself and your relationship with Jesus Christ?

Which "My Action" of the week brought you great joy or difficulty? Why?

Please journal your thoughts. (Space is available on the next page for journaling.)

# Genesis 24:1-27

Third Monday of Lent

Genesis 24:1-67 captures the love story of Rebekah and Isaac. The story begins when Abraham instructs his chief servant, Eliezer, to find a wife for Isaac. Abraham is adamant that Isaac marries within the family to avoid intermarriage with their pagan neighbors.

Eliezer travels to Northwest Mesopotamia with his caravan of camels and goods from Abraham's land. At the well, Eliezer asks God for a sign to let him know which young woman was to be Isaac's future bride. When Rebekah comes to the well, not only did she give Eliezer a drink of water, but she offered a drink of water to Eliezer's camels. Rebekah's actions aligned with the prayer that Eliezer prayed, confirming that God had chosen Rebekah for Isaac. Rebekah's servant heart is clearly demonstrated by her actions at the well.

When asked to help someone in need, do you take the initiative? Do you have a servant spirit? Our Lord and Savior demonstrates for us the servant's heart. Jesus explains to his disciples that their practice of servant leadership is to be different from their self-serving leadership style. Jesus says, "Just as the Son of Man did not come to be served, but to serve and to give his life as a ransom." Jesus' mission was to serve others and to give his life away. Our mission is to be an imitator of Jesus Christ and to give our life away. A popular gospel song entitled "I Give Myself Away," recorded by William McDowell, describes our servanthood posture:

> *I give myself away*
> *I give myself away*
> *So You can use me (Repeat)*
> **(Verse 1)**
> *Here I am*
> *Here I stand*
> *Lord my life is in Your hands*
> *Lord I'm longing to see*
> *Your desires revealed in me.*
> **(Bridge)**
> *My life is not my own*
> *To you I belong*
> *I give myself*
> *I give myself to You (Repeat)*[26]

Servant leaders value the work and worth of others. According to Ken Blanchard, the five most prominent servant leadership characteristics are valuing people, humility, listening, trust, and caring.[27] I believe that the benefits of servant leadership allow us to build deeper trust in our relationships, encourage creativity among others,

---

26 William McDowell, "I Give Myself Away," 2009. Lyrics © Fun Attic Music, LLC.

27 resources.kenblanchard.com/blanchard-leaderchat/the-top-5-characteristics-of-servant-leaders

and produce positive results. When was the last time you took the initiative to address a felt need? What was the outcome of the project?

## Selected Scriptures

- Mark 10:42-45

- John 13:12-15

- Acts 20:35

## Prayer

O Lord, give me a heart to serve humanity. Amen.

## Reflection

Do you normally take the initiative when you see or hear of a need? Why or why not?

Identify servant leaders in your church or community. What are their common characteristics? List them.

## My Action

Identify servant leaders in your church or community and host a luncheon or dinner to show your appreciation for their work.

# DAY EIGHTEEN
# Psalm 81

Third Tuesday of Lent

As a child, I never had a problem being obedient to my parents. I guess you would say I was a "rule follower." I now understand that humans struggle with the word *obedience*. Humanity cannot exist without some form of obedience to law and order. Moreover, the Bible is full of words that express or suggest obedience.

In the *New Revised Standard Version* (NRSV), forms of the word group *obey/disobey* occur 283 times.[28] However, when combined with related words that imply *obedience* (*lay, command, commandment, king, ruler*), the number increases to 6,302.[29] In addition, many biblical passages deal with the subject of *obey/disobedience* beginning with the fall of humanity. In the Old Testament, the most common word for *obedience* is *shama*, which means *hearken*. In the New Testament, twenty-four words can be translated by some form of the *obey/disobey* word group.[30]

---

28 Sakenfeld, Katharine D., General Editor, *The New Interpreter's Dictionary of the Bible, Me-R, Volume 4,* (Nashville: Abingdon Press, 2009), p. 314.

29 Ibid.

30 Ibid.

It is the essential being and character of God, as God the Creator and Redeemer, that defines the biblical concept of *obedience*.[31]

In today's reading, Psalm 81 begins as a psalm of praise that was written specifically for the Jewish festival—perhaps the Feast of Tabernacles celebrated by the Israelites. This festival commemorated the wilderness wanderings for forty years and the promise to provide for their daily needs. The second half of the psalm invites Israel to listen and obey God. This act of obedience allows God to protect them and pour out blessings upon them.

## Selected Scriptures

- Exodus 2:23

- Psalm 50:7

- Deuteronomy 32:14

## Prayer

O Lord, thank you for your Word that I promise to obey. Amen.

---

31 Ibid.

## Reflection

What lessons can we learn from the failures of the
Israelites?

When we are stubborn or disobedient to God's Word, what
happens to our lives?

## My Action

Jesus Christ is the only person without sin. Meditate on
Philippians 2:8. What does the scripture mean to you?
Journal your thoughts.

## DAY NINETEEN
# Jeremiah 2:4-13

Third Wednesday of Lent

Estimates suggest that in 2022 U.S. adults will spend an average of three hours watching television daily.[32] According to the latest data, the average amount of time spent on social media worldwide is two hours and 27 minutes.[33] Have we allowed our favorite pastimes to prevent us from having a relationship with God? Have we forsaken our relationship with God? Is our relationship with God a priority?

As we examine our text for today, the prophet Jeremiah is reminding the Israelites of God's faithfulness, emphasizing God's love for them, and reminding them that, at one time, they were close to God. However, in verse 13, God speaks through Jeremiah, "My people have committed two sins: they have forsaken me, the spring of living water and have dug their own cisterns, broken cisterns that cannot hold water."

---

32 https://www.statista.com/statistics/186833/average-television-use-per-person-in-the-us-since-2002.

33 https://www.oberlo.com/statistics/how-much-time-does-the-average-person-spend-on-social-media.

In biblical times, a cistern was an artificial reservoir that was dug into the earth or carved into rock for collecting and storing water.[34] Israel had long dry seasons, so the ability to keep fresh water in cisterns was crucial. Therefore, fresh water was extremely valuable, and a broken cistern was useless. The prophet Jeremiah used the illustration of "broken cisterns" to point out the extreme foolishness of God's people, Israel.[35] This message gave a reprimand to people who were no longer committed to God, a message which applies to believers today.

Jeremiah prophesied in a day when the people of Judah had abandoned God and were no longer depending on God to supply their needs. Jeremiah 2 reveals they had created cisterns of idolatry and immorality for themselves, hoping that the pleasures of those sins could satisfy their needs.[36] Interestingly, the Israelites quickly discovered that the cisterns they made were broken and could never quench their spiritual thirst. Jeremiah accused them of committing two sins in verse 13: they had forsaken God, and their cisterns were cracked and could not hold water.

Is it possible today that believers have abandoned God? Are we looking for God in our careers, our financial portfolios, or our political associations? Have we built "cisterns" that will never be able to quench our thirst because we are not spending quality time cultivating our relationship with God?

---

34 "Broken Cisterns," www.growingchristians.org.

35 Ibid.

36 Ibid.

## Selected Scriptures

- Isaiah 55:1-2

- John 4:10-14

- John 6:35

## Prayer

O Lord, let me not forsake you for the hustle and grind of the day. Let me drink from the living water that never runs dry. Amen.

## Reflection

The average person spends an enormous amount of time on their cell phones but little time reading scripture. How do we improve on the spiritual disciplines of reading God's Word when phone apps are so accessible?

Reflect and identify your personal "cisterns."

## My Action

During this week, fast from your favorite pastime and replace it with reading God's Word.

# Ephesians 4:25-32

Fourth Thursday of Lent

*Do not let unwholesome talk come out of your
mouths, but only what is helpful for building
others up according to their needs that it may
benefit those who listen.*

*Ephesians 4:29*

As a trained biologist, it always amazes me that the pink
muscular organ in the mouth of human beings used for
tasting, licking, swallowing, and articulating words can
build up or tear down a person's self-esteem in a matter of
seconds. How many times have we heard of someone who
said, texted, or tweeted inappropriate words? Inappropriate
words can make the headline news, expose victims to
racial slurs, and break up relationships.

James 3:8-10 says:

*But no human being can tame the tongue. It is
a restless evil full of deadly poison. With the
tongue, we praise our Lord and Father, and
with it, we curse human beings, who have been
made in God's likeness. Out of the same mouth
come praise and cursing.*

The reflection for today admonishes us to not let foul or abusive language come out of our mouths. I believe everything we say should be good, helpful, and encouraging to those who hear. Jesus states in Mark 7:15, "Nothing outside a person can defile them by going into them. Rather, it is what comes out of a person that defiles them." Words can be a powerful tool to bless or curse, hurt or heal.

## Selected Scriptures

- Proverbs 18:21

- Psalm 34:13

- Colossians 3:16

## Prayer

O Lord, guard my tongue and help me to know what to say and when to say it. Amen.

## Reflection

Have you ever offended someone with your words? What did you say? What did you learn about the power of words? How did you rectify your mistake?

## My Action

Reflect on the "Seven Last Words" of Christ on the cross:

*"Father, forgive them, for they know not what they do."*

*"Truly, I say to you, today you will be with me in paradise."*

*"Woman, behold your son! Behold, your mother!"*

*"My God, my God, why have you forsaken me?"*

*"I thirst."*

*"It is finished."*

*"Father, into thy hands I commend my spirit."*

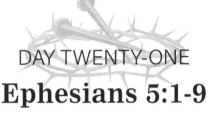

# Ephesians 5:1-9

Fourth Friday of Lent

According to Google, an *imitator* is a person who copies the behavior or actions of another. The word *imitate* suggests following a model or a pattern. The Apostle Paul states in today's text, "Be imitators of God, therefore as dearly loved children." I believe, just as children grow up imitating their parents, favorite sports figures, or role models, we should grow up imitating Jesus Christ. We are to follow the model of Christ's actions revealed in the Gospel of Luke 9:23-26, "Then He said to them all: 'Whoever wants to be my disciple must deny themselves and take up their cross daily and follow me.'"

*To deny yourself* in the original Greek-to-English translation means to disregard one's own interest. The problem with denying yourself is that we currently live in a culture that promotes the "ME" syndrome. To deny yourself doesn't mean to reject your own identity but to lose your self-centeredness. Dietrich Bonhoeffer, a martyr during Hitler's times, writes in his book *The Cost of Discipleship* that when Jesus calls a man or woman, he bids him to come and die. To deny yourself means to die to one's appetites, cravings, and desires and to be obedient to God's will made known through Jesus Christ.

The Apostle Paul instructs us in Romans 8:5, "For those who live according to the flesh, set their minds on the things of the flesh, but those who live according to the Spirit, the things of the Spirit."

As believers, we must surrender our wills, thoughts, and emotions. To "take up our cross" means to publicly identify with Christ, to experience certain opposition, and to be committed to facing suffering for Christ's sake. Jesus, in carrying his cross, illustrated the ultimate submission required of his followers. Jesus states in Luke 14:27, "Whoever does not carry their cross and follow me cannot be my disciple."

Our life is to be a life of surrender, suffering, sacrifice, and service. In the original Greek language, the phrase "follow me" is in the present imperative tense, which means there is a continuous action. What Jesus is teaching in the text is, "Let my disciples follow me continually." As believers, we must walk in the steps of Jesus. When you follow Jesus, there will be favor and blessings in your life.

Jesus didn't tell us to follow his shadow. He told us to follow his glory. Jesus wants us to follow him rather than lead a life of sin and self-satisfaction.

The text also explains that to imitate Jesus Christ, we must "live a life of love, just as Christ loved us and gave himself up for us as a fragrant offering and sacrifice to God." Love is the heart of the Christian faith, which is revealed throughout the Word of God. As imitators, believers should demonstrate the same type of self-sacrificial love.

*Love* is an action word. Love is a way of living that is made possible by God's grace through the working of the Holy Spirit. The entire Gospel message focuses on love. John 3:16 reminds us, "For God so loved the world that he gave his one and only Son, that whoever believes in him shall not perish but have eternal life."

Our fragrant offering to God must demonstrate our love for Jesus Christ by accepting Christ as our personal Lord and Savior. "For we are to God the pleasing aroma of Christ among those who are being saved and those who are perishing" (2 Corinthians 2:15).

## Selected Scriptures

- 1 Peter 2:21
- Philippians 2:3-8
- Galatians 1:4

## Prayer

O Lord, teach me how to model my life after you. Amen.

## Reflection

What characteristics of Jesus Christ would you like to imitate? List them and explain why.

Reflect on the thought that "love is a response." How do we show that love is a response?

## My Action

Write a love letter to Jesus Christ. Include in the letter the characteristics that you would like to imitate.

## DAY TWENTY-TWO
# John 1:1-9

Fourth Saturday of Lent

John 1:1-18, known as "The Prologue," has become the spiritual tenet of the Christian doctrine. The Christian doctrine is known as the Trinity, where God is one being in three distinct persons. In verse 1, Jesus is referred to as "the Word," from the Greek word *logos*.[37] In this gospel, John provides clear proof that Jesus is the Son of God and that, by believing in him, we may have eternal life. Jesus, the Word of God, is the One through whom we hear God's voice. He is the One in whom we meet and welcome God into our lives.[38]

At an early age, I had a hunger and thirst for reading the Word. I came to love the Bible stories that I learned in Sunday school and Vacation Bible School. Little did I know that accepting a call to ministry was in my future. Interestingly, I am the fourteenth clergy person in my family; fourteen individuals in my family have answered God's call to serve the church and to minister to God's people.

---

37 http://www.bibleref.com/John.

38 Richards, Lawrence O., *Devotional Commentary,* (Colorado Springs: Cook Communications Ministries, 2002), p. 758.

As I studied the Bible, I began to realize that Jesus was the embodiment of the Word of God. I learned at an early age that words like *love, forgiveness, repentance, redemption,* and *salvation* all pointed back to Jesus Christ. The Word became my source of inspiration and guidance for life issues. If I struggled with a life issue, I could always find solace and direction in the Word of God. I began to depend on God's *logos* Word to get me through the day and God's *rhema* Word to reveal the hidden gems in God's Word. The crucial elements I have learned from the Word are that there is:

- No promise God can't keep
- No problem God can't solve
- No pain God can't comfort
- No prayer God can't answer

In the text, John taught me that human life is lived in light or darkness. The darkness of evil will never overtake the light of Christ. Jesus Christ is the creator of life, and Jesus brings light to humanity. In the light, we see ourselves as sinners saved by grace through faith. Matthew 5:16 reminds us, "Let your light shine before others, that they may see your good deeds and praise your Father in heaven."

Finally, the text reveals that John the Baptist is the forerunner to prepare the disciples for Jesus Christ's arrival.

## Selected Scriptures

- 1 John 1:1-2

- John 3:19

- Matthew 3:1

## Prayer

O Lord, teach me your Word so I may live an abundant life. Amen.

## Reflection

What have you learned about yourself when you study the Word of God?

Reflect on the text; "I have hidden your word in my heart that I might not sin against you" (Psalm 119:11). What does this passage of scripture mean to you?

## My Action

Memorize 2 Timothy 3:16-17:

> *All Scripture is God-breathed and is useful for teaching, rebuking, correcting and training in righteousness, so that the servant of God may be thoroughly equipped for every good work.*

# Fourth Sunday in Lent

**My Personal Reflection Notes**

*Reflect on this past week.*

What day stood out during this week's Lenten journey?

What did you learn about yourself and your relationship with Jesus Christ?

Which "My Action" of the week brought you great joy or difficulty? Why?

Please journal your thoughts. (Space is available on the next page for journaling.)

# DAY TWENTY-THREE
## Acts 9:1-20

Fourth Monday of Lent

George Barna, founder of the Barna Group, a research firm that specializes in studying religious beliefs and behaviors of Americans, states that we encounter seven unchurched people daily. Who will you encounter today? A co-worker, a doctor, or a clerk at the grocery store? When people encounter you, do they walk away encouraged or discouraged?

Saul's road-to-Damascus encounter is one of my favorite Bible stories. This story is vastly popular because it is mentioned three times in the book of Acts (9:1-9a, 22:6-16, and 26:12-18). Saul (later known as Paul) refers to this encounter as the start of his new life in Christ. "Am I not free? Am I not an apostle? Have I not seen Jesus our Lord?" (1 Corinthians 9:1). In a blink of an eye, Saul the persecutor becomes Paul the preacher. Saul is both converted and commissioned.[39] He is converted to being a disciple and commissioned by the Lord to proclaim the Lord's name. The story reveals how Saul acknowledges

---

39 Collins Kenneth J., and Robert W. Wall, *Wesley One Volume Commentary,* (Nashville: Abingdon Press, 2020), p. 695.

Jesus as Savior, confesses his sin, surrenders his life, and vows to obey him.

There are two especially distinct moments in my life when I encountered Jesus Christ: when I accepted Jesus Christ at Brannen Chapel United Methodist Church at the age of twelve and when I accepted my call to ministry at Ben Hill United Methodist Church.

I vividly remember the day at Brannen Chapel. I was sitting in church with my dad, and Rev. George Bradley "opened the doors" for Christian discipleship. I remember taking that first step that landed me in front of Rev. Bradley. He leaned over the altar rail and whispered in my ear, "Do you know what you are doing?" This was the first day ever in my life that I thought an adult was stupid! I whispered back, "Yes, I come to accept Jesus for myself."

Little did Pastor Bradley know that my relationship with Jesus took place long before I walked down the aisle that day. The feeling of pure joy that Jesus was my Lord and Savior came over me. The pastor and congregation were amazed, but my parents stood proud as I accepted Christ for myself.

On Sunday, February 13, 1994, at the 11:45 a.m. worship service, student minister Michael T. McQueen was preaching from Ephesians 4:11-13, and the title of the sermon was "Are You Called?" At the end of the sermon, Minister McQueen offered an altar call to come and pray. As I knelt at the altar, I heard the Lord speak: "Sharma, go preach my Word."

The flood of tears that covered my face and the single-hand confirmation on my shoulders by the late Rev. Valerie Earvin overwhelmed me. To witness the entire church standing behind me was another sacred moment I will never forget.

The word *encounter*, defined by Google, is an unexpected experience. Saul, the persecutor of Christians, didn't encounter just anyone; he encountered the risen Savior. Sharma, the 12-year-old child and the 30-year-old woman didn't encounter just anyone; she encountered her Lord and Savior.

Have you had a personal encounter with the Lord Jesus? Were you praying at the altar in search of answers? Saul's encounter with the Lord changed the rest of his life. The one who was out to persecute those who called on the name (verse 14) was the one who went forth to bear the name (verses 15-16).

## Selected Scriptures

- Acts 8:1-3

- Acts 19:23

- Acts 26:12-18

## Prayer

O Lord, I long for a Damascus Road experience. Amen.

## Reflection

When was the first time you encountered Jesus Christ?

What did you experience? How did your life change when you encountered Jesus Christ?

## My Action

Journal your encounter with Jesus Christ.

# DAY TWENTY-FOUR
# Psalm 146
## Fourth Tuesday of Lent

According to *Nelson's Bible Dictionary*, "Praise is an act of worship or acknowledgment by which the virtues or deeds of another are recognized and extolled."

In seminary, studying under Dr. Melva Costen, I learned to appreciate praise and worship. Life struggles and experiences taught me how to praise and worship God. There have been times in my life when hearing a praise song, listening to an old hymn, or recalling words in a song helped me make it through the day.

My mom had a Sunday ritual to wake us up; she always—and I mean always—played the song "May the Work I've Done Speak for Me." When we planned my mom's eulogy, it was only fitting to have someone sing her favorite song in the service. Although my mom was an avid singer and listener of hymns, I taught her to appreciate contemporary praise music. She taught me to appreciate the meaning of the hymns.

Todd Gaddis, author of *Seven Reasons to Praise the Lord*, warns that we must not wait and look back wondering why we didn't praise God more. He suggests that the seven reasons to praise God are as follows:

- The Bible commands it.
- Praise facilitates access to God.
- Praise is where God lives.
- Praise promotes productivity.
- Praise chases away despair.
- Praise is an effective weapon against the devil.
- God is worthy of it.[40]

Gaddis' article resonates with my Christian journey—especially the last three reasons.

- **Praise chases away despair.** When I was recovering from my four hip surgeries in 2018-2019, there was nothing better to chase my pain away than a praise song that allowed me to focus on God and not myself. Motives for praising God include and cover almost every aspect of human existence and also plant and animal life.[41] Praise allows humans the opportunity to move beyond themselves—their needs, fears, and hopes—and to return something to their Creator and Redeemer.[42]

- **Praise is an effective weapon against the enemy.** I believe that Satan can't compete with sincere praise to God. Praise destroys Satan by tearing down the enemy and building up our confidence in the Lord.

---

40 https://research.lifeway.com.seven.

41 Ibid.

42 Sakenfeld, Katharine D., General Editor, *The New Interpreter's Dictionary of the Bible, Me-R Volume 4*, (Nashville: Abingdon Press, 2009), p. 578.

- **The Lord is worthy of our praise.** Praise is motivated by gratitude for God's actions in the world as well as wonder and awe at God's qualities of creativeness, justice, everlasting love, and joy over God's saving actions.[43]

Psalm 146 begins a series of five final songs known as the "hallelujah psalms."[44] Each of the psalms begins and ends with "Praise the Lord!" Interestingly, the psalmist alternates poetically between heaven and earth. The primary focus of this psalm is to encourage the people to praise and trust the Lord.

The structure of Psalm 146:1-4 depicts the reliability of God and, unfortunately, our fallibility. The psalmist reminds us in verses 5-9 about the blessings of trusting God by pointing out that God keeps God's promises, upholds the oppressed, feeds the hungry, frees the prisoners, gives sight to the blind, protects the foreigners, and cares for the orphans and widows.

## Selected Scriptures

- Psalm 147
- Psalm 148
- Psalm 149

43 Ibid.

44 https://enduringword.com.Psalm146, David Guzik.

## Prayer

O Lord, Praise the Lord! How excellent is your name in all the earth! Amen.

## Reflection

What are your motives in praising God?

What happens to you when you praise God? Does praising God sometimes move you to tears? Are you sensitive to your surroundings? What do you feel?

## My Action

Write a poem of praise to God and put the poem to music.

DAY TWENTY-FIVE

# Matthew 9:27-34

Fourth Wednesday of Lent

A miracle story normally has five characteristics:

- A problem or crisis that always gets worse
- Development of the crisis
- Contact between key individuals
- Healing
- Public confirmation

According to scholars, the Gospel of Matthew includes more miracle stories than any other gospel. As we examine the text for today, the story of the two blind men is interwoven within the story of the demon-possessed man, a biblical technique called *intercalation*. This story's problem, or crisis, is that three men in need of healing confront Jesus.

The development of the crisis occurs when the two blind men persistently approach Jesus. Jesus doesn't immediately respond to their plea but waits to see if they have faith to believe he can heal them. Unlike the two blind men, however, the demon-possessed man is physically brought to Jesus.

The key individuals in this text are Jesus—referred to as the "Son of David"—the three men, a crowd that stood in amazement of the miracle, and the Pharisees who always challenged Jesus' authority and ministry.

The two blind men and the demon-possessed man are healed from their infirmities. In biblical times, regardless of the person or situation—whether they were young or old, rich or poor, man or woman, sinner or saint, Jew or Gentile—Jesus was not afraid to heal or touch the "untouchables."

In both cases, Jesus commands them to keep their healing a secret. However, all three men disobey Jesus, and the news spread all over the region. The crowd that witnesses the demon-possessed man is amazed, "Nothing like this has ever been seen in Israel." However, the Pharisees say, "It is by the prince of demons that he drives out demons." In Matthew 9, the Pharisees accuse Jesus of four different sins: befriending outcasts, blasphemy, irreverence, and serving Satan. The Pharisees only see evil at work; they are not willing to admit the miraculous power of Jesus Christ.

Jesus poses a threat to the Pharisees because he weakens their control, challenges their beliefs, and exposes their insincere motives. Instead of Jesus responding to the accusation of serving Satan, he resumes his ministry of preaching, teaching, and healing.

Did the Pharisees purposely cast doubt that Jesus could really heal? Do we believe that our Lord and Savior is still in the miracle-working ministry?

I stand as a living witness that not only Jesus can heal, but miracles still happen if you believe. When people ask me if I believe in miracles, my answer is a resounding YES! Why? Because you're looking at a miracle.

## Selected Scriptures

- Matthew 12:24

- Mark 7:36

- Mark 10:46-47

## Prayer

O Lord, touch me and heal me with your mighty power. Amen.

## Reflection

Do you believe that God can help you? What is your evidence?

Have you ever witnessed a miracle in your life or someone else's life? What happened? Reflect on the miracle story.

## My Action

Read several miracle stories in the gospel and see if you can recognize the five unique characteristics of a miracle story.

# Ezekiel 1:1-3, 2:8-3:3

## Fifth Thursday of Lent

Dr. Norman Habel, an Old Testament scholar, believes that "a call" is a summons by God to carry out a particular function.[45] He describes four commonly displayed stages in a divine call displayed throughout the biblical stories.[46] He suggests that the call upon our lives has a direct correlation to these stages.[47]

Habel believes:

- There is a divine confrontation by God.
- There is the rejection of the call.
- There is the assurance that God will be with you always.
- There is acceptance of the call, which leads to various responses.[48]

The book named after the prophet Ezekiel begins with a dated call narrative told by the prophet himself in the

---

45 Lewis, Sharma D. *Journey to Transformation,* (Knoxville: Market Square Books, 2020), p. 113.

46 Ibid.

47 Ibid.

48 Ibid.

first person.[49] After a broad introductory description of a *theophany* comes the sending and commissioning of the prophet (1:1-3,15).[50] A *theophany* is any direct visual manifestation of the presence of God.[51]

In today's devotion, Ezekiel saw the glory of God in a vision and was called to speak God's Word to God's rebellious people. Interestingly, the reluctant Ezekiel ate a scroll containing God's Word and was warned again that the Israelites would not listen.[52] Eating the scroll symbolized digesting and applying the Word of God.[53]

If there is ever a time to study, know, and apply the Word of God to our lives, the time is now. Reading the Bible daily provides several benefits. The Bible reveals to us the character of God and shows us God's revelation of God's self to humanity. In the Bible, we experience God's holiness, faithfulness, grace, mercy, and loving character.

As you reflect on this Lenten season, what has God called you to do? Has God called you out of your comfort zones to love the unlovable? Has God called you to share your faith with others? I believe that God calls individuals, ministries, and churches. Henry Blackaby, author of *Experiencing God*, believes that God is constantly at work

---

49 Zimmerli, Walter. *A Commentary on the Book of the Prophet Ezekiel,* Chapters 1-24, (Philadelphia: Fortress Press, 1979), p. 1.

50 Ibid.

51 Youngblood, Ronald F., General Editor, *Nelson's New Illustrated Bible Dictionary,* (Nashville: Thomas Nelson Publishers, 1995), p. 1242.

52 Richard, Lawrence O., *Devotional Commentary,* (Colorado Springs: Cook Communications Ministries, 2002), p. 483.

53 Ibid.

around us. He believes that when we hear God's call and respond appropriately, there is no limit to what God can do in and through God's people.

The Apostle Paul writes in Ephesians 4:11-13:

> *It was He who gave some to be apostles, some to be prophets, some to be evangelists, some to be pastors and teachers, to prepare God's people for the works of service so that the body of Christ may be built up until we all reach unity in the faith and in the knowledge of the Son of God and become mature, attaining to the whole measure of the fullness of Christ.*

We must understand that before we existed on earth, God was shaping us for God's purpose. God knows us intimately and intricately, every detail and nuance. God took the time to form each of us precious in God's sight despite our faults. God uses ordinary people to do extraordinary things for the Kingdom of God.

## Selected Scriptures

- Jeremiah 1:11-16

- Isaiah 6:5-8

- Ezekiel 8:4

## Prayer

O Lord, help me to accept and walk in my divine call. Amen.

## Reflection

Do you feel that God has a call on your life for ministry? What biblical person aligns with your call? Why?

Have you experienced the four stages of a call suggested by Dr. Norman Habel? Currently, what stage do you feel that you are in?

## My Action

Read and reflect on the following call stories in the Bible:

- Moses – Exodus 3:1-12

- Deborah – Judges 4:4-22

- Peter –Luke 5:1-11

- Mary – Luke 1

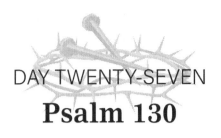

# Psalm 130

Fifth Friday of Lent

The Bible reminds us in 1 John 1:9, "If we confess our sins, he is faithful and just and will forgive us our sins and purify us from all unrighteousness." God's desire for God's children is that we confess, seek forgiveness, and repent from our sins. God allowed his son, Jesus, to die for our sins so that God could offer us forgiveness.

Similar to 1 John 1:9, Psalm 130's primary focus is that God will surely forgive us if we confess our sins to God. The psalmist confidently encourages Israel to do as he has done—confess. Some scholars believe that Psalm 130, normally noted as anonymous, was actually written by Hezekiah. This psalm is also one of the seven penitential psalms used to engage the reader in the disciplines of forgiveness and repentance.

Scholars share that John Wesley, founder of Methodism, heard Psalm 130 sung on the afternoon before his "strangely warmed" experience at Aldersgate. Psalm 130, also classified as "a song of ascents," constitutes a series of pilgrimage songs that stress trust in God and regard the temple as the locus of worship and blessing.[54]

Psalm 130 contains four parts that are unified by the connecting elements of forgiveness. The structure of Psalm 130 begins with an individual prayer for help: "Out of the depths I cry to you, O Lord; O Lord, hear my voice. Let your ears be attentive to my cry for mercy."

When I read these two verses, I can only remember hearing George Floyd crying for his mother. Can we imagine that, in the same breath that George Floyd cried out to God, the psalmist gives voice to our cry?

The song then shifts, and in verses 3-4, the psalmist points out, "If you, O Lord, kept a record of sins, O Lord, who could stand? But with you there is forgiveness; therefore you are feared."

Isn't it reassuring to know that God doesn't keep a record of our sins and that when God forgives, God forgives completely? Then the psalmist's confession of faith takes the form of waiting in hope for the Lord (verses 5-6).[55] Finally, the psalm ends with an appeal for the entire community to hope in the Lord with the same steadfast resolution as the psalmist (verses 7-8).[56]

---

54 Sakenfeld, Katharine D., General Editor, *The New Interpreter's Dictionary of the Bible, Me-R, Volume 4*, (Nashville: Abingdon Press, 2009), p. 677.

55 Mays, James L., Editor, *Interpretation A Bible Commentary for Teaching and Preaching*, (Louisville: John Knox Press, 1994), p. 405.

56 Gaventa, Beverly Roberts and David Petersen, Editors, *The New Interpreter's Bible, One Volume Commentary*, (Nashville: Abingdon Press, 2010), p. 345.

## Selected Scriptures

- Psalm 33:18-22
- Isaiah 40:31
- Isaiah 51:5

## Prayer

O Lord, out of my sins, I cry out to you. Please forgive me, O Lord. Amen.

## Reflection

"The Lord keeps no record of our sins." How does this knowledge motivate you to be in a right relationship with the Lord?

What does it mean when you hear "forgiveness is of the Lord"?

## My Action

Read and meditate on the seven penitential psalms:

- Psalm 6
- Psalm 32
- Psalm 38
- Psalm 51
- Psalm 102
- Psalm 130
- Psalm 143

# Luke 1:26-28

## Fifth Saturday of Lent
### Annunciation of the Lord

The Annunciation is a Christian holiday commemorating the visit of the angel Gabriel to the Virgin Mary, where he announces that she will give birth to Jesus Christ.[57]

Have you ever wondered why Mary was "chosen" to be the mother of Jesus Christ? According to *Webster's Dictionary*, the word *chosen* is defined as being "selected or marked for favor or special privilege." Another definition reveals that the term *chosen* is "one who is the object of choice or an elected person."

As our text tells us, in the sixth month, the angel Gabriel approaches Mary and gives her the most shocking message of her life. The angel says, "Rejoice highly favored one; the Lord is with you; blessed are you among women." Then the angel continues, "Do not be afraid, Mary, for you have found favor with God and behold you will conceive and bring forth a Son and you shall name Him Jesus." Of course, Mary is startled, and she questions the angel, "How can this be since I do not know a man?"

Mary is chosen because she has favor with God.

---

57 https://nationaltoday.com/feast-of-the-annunciation.

According to *Vine's Expository Dictionary*, the Greek word for *favor* means "freely bestowed." When God has favor upon you, you can call your creditors, and they will help you work out your financial problem. When God has favor upon you, God can make the impossible possible.

Secondly, Mary is chosen because she is faithful. According to Hebrews 11:1 in the *Contemporary English Version* (CEV), "Faith is the reality of what we hope for, the proof of what we don't see."

Mary is willing to be utilized by God to bring the light-bearer into the world. She could have opposed her role, but she accepts the honor from God. Mary knows that she will be criticized and experience slander, despair, and loneliness. She knows that people will gossip and that she will be excluded from her community because pregnancy before marriage is a serious offense in her culture. Mary overcame her fears with faith.

Finally, Mary is chosen because God fulfills God's promise through her. God can work through natural processes to achieve God's will, and God worked in a special way to allow the Virgin Mary to conceive. Isaiah 9:6, "For to us a child is born, to us a son is given, and the government will be on his shoulders. And he will be called Wonderful Counselor, Mighty God, Everlasting Father, Prince of Peace."

## Selected Scriptures

- Matthew 2:21-23

- Matthew 19:26

- Hebrews 11:1-6

## Prayer

O Lord, please grant me favor in your sight and use me for your glory. Amen.

## Reflection

What does it mean "to be favored by God?"

Mary was faithful. How have you been faithful to God on your Christian journey?

## My Action

Read the story of Joseph. Journal the ways God favors Joseph.

# Fifth Sunday in Lent

## My Personal Reflection Notes

*Reflect on this past week.*

What day stood out during this week's Lenten journey?

What did you learn about yourself and your relationship with Jesus Christ?

Which "My Action" of the week brought you great joy or difficulty? Why?

Please journal your thoughts.

## DAY TWENTY-NINE
# 1 Kings 17:17-24

Fifth Monday of Lent

What does it mean for us as believers to walk by faith? As believers, whether we are experiencing great joy or serious pain, how do we walk by faith?

Our faith affects how we live and walk with God. Faith is so central to my being; it means clinging to the hope that God will eventually come through in my personal situation. The adult choir often sang these poignant words at Brannen Chapel UMC:

> *We've come this far by faith*
> *Leaning on the Lord*
> *Trusting in His Holy Word*
> *He never failed me yet*
> *Oh, can't turn around*
> *We've come this far by faith.*

This song became the hallmark of our church. Still today, when I struggle with my own life issues, I can hear this song resonate in my ears.

Walking by faith is believing even when you can't see it. The faith of the widow from Zarephath is first challenged with the visit of the prophet Elijah when she is asked to go and prepare food for him. Her faith is rewarded because the "bin of flour was not used up, nor did the jar of oil run dry" (1 Kings 17:16). Her faith is again challenged when her son becomes ill and eventually stops breathing.

The Zarephath widow laments to Elijah that her son died because of her sinfulness. The text reveals that Elijah is present to ask God to restore her son to life. The Zarephath woman couldn't see the resurrection of her son. The lesson learned is just because you can't see it with the naked eye doesn't mean that it doesn't exist.

The Word of God reminds us in 2 Corinthians 5:7, "For we walk by faith, not by sight" (NKJV). Faith is visualizing the future. True faith is characterized by a forward look and an openness to the pull of the future that God has planned. Hebrews 11:1, "Faith makes us sure of what we hope for and gives us proof of what we cannot see" (CEB). The world wants us to believe that we must "see" before we believe.

Secondly, walking by faith means obeying even when you don't understand. In your life, has God given you an assignment that doesn't make sense? For example, to return to school at an older age, quit your job and change careers, or move to a new city? The Zarephath widow didn't understand Elijah's request for food, and she didn't understand when Elijah commands, "Give me your son." Then he cries out to the Lord, "O Lord my God, have you brought tragedy also upon this widow I am staying with, by causing her son to die?" Because of the widow's obedience, the starving woman is fed daily, and her son is restored.

Abram, at the age of 75, is another example of obeying

when he didn't understand why. In Genesis 12, God tells Abram to pack his bags, gather his family and possessions, and depart from his home.

Like the widow and Abram, we, too, must learn to trust and obey God—even when it seems to make no sense.

Finally, walking by faith is also to persist even when you don't know the outcome. The Zarephath widow was angry at Elijah as she pointed to her own sinfulness being the reason for her son's death. However, she persists in asking the prophet to heal her son.

Recording artist, ordained minister, and author Judy Jacobs states in her book, *Take It by Force! Faith that Stands Firm in the Face of Opposition,* that believers must develop an attitude of what she calls "violent faith." She describes that "violent faith" is sheer determination, aggressiveness in the Spirit, and an attitude of perseverance. She further states that there will always be opposition to your mission and purpose in life, but the key to persistence is to keep your eyes fixed on Jesus. Faith is believing, despite your circumstances and surroundings. Faith is relinquishing trust in oneself and putting your trust in God. The return of the widow's son to life is the final proof that God truly lived and spoke through the prophet Elijah.

## Selected Scriptures

- 2 Kings 4:32-35
- Hebrews 11:6
- Hebrews 11:35

## Prayer

O Lord, help me to walk by faith in believing, obeying, and trusting in your Word. Amen.

## Reflection

How have you been persistent in living a faithful life for God?

What does it mean, "Obedience is better than sacrifice"?

## My Action

Read 2 Kings 4:8-37 about the Shunammite woman's son who was restored to life. Then read 1 Kings 17:17-24 about the Zarephath woman's son who was also resurrected. Record the similarities and differences between these two stories.

# 2 Kings 4:18-37

Fifth Tuesday of Lent

Acts 20:35 states, "It is more blessed to give than to receive." When I was a child, my mother and father would often repeat this scripture to my siblings and me. At first, I really didn't understand the meaning of this passage. However, as I grew older and witnessed the giving spirit of both my parents, I actually wanted and prayed for the spirit of generosity. As long as I can remember, I witnessed my parents giving back to our church, the community, and the people in any capacity that was needed. Not only did my parents help many people, but their acts of generosity brought a sense of joy to their lives.

Today's devotion centers around a wealthy woman from Shunem who showed Elisha generosity. As a result of her generosity, she is blessed with an unexpected son who dies and is then restored to life.

There are two life lessons in the text for us to heed:

1. Use your gifts and resources to be a blessing to others.
2. Be satisfied with what God has blessed you with in your life.

One of the first lessons in the text about the Shunammite woman is that she used what she had to be a blessing to Elisha. At first, she shares her generosity by preparing a meal for Elisha when he visits her home. Her hospitality continues as she regularly prepares meals whenever he visits.

After his frequent visits, she asks her husband to prepare a room for Elisha. "I know that this man who often comes our way is a holy man of God. Let's make a small room on the roof and put in it a bed and a table, a chair and a lamp for him." Just as the wealthy woman used what she had to bless and provide for Elisha, we, too, must use our gifts and resources to bless and help others.

How many times have you sacrificed to be a blessing to others? We must also recognize that we may not be able to build a room for someone in our house, but God sees what we have and recognizes what we can give. Matthew 10:42 (NLT) states, "And if you give even a cup of cold water to one of the least of my followers, you will surely be rewarded." The spirit of giving directs our attention and heart to Jesus Christ, leading to an increase of joy and a more intimate relationship with Christ.

The second lesson for us to learn in the text is to be satisfied with what God has blessed you with in your life. This does not mean that we should not strive for better things in life but that the blessing of contentment is important.

Elisha said to Gehazi, the servant:

> *Tell her, "You have gone to all this trouble for us.*
> *Now what can be done for you? Can we speak on*
> *your behalf to the king or the commander of the*
> *army?" She replied, "I have a home among my*
> *own people."*
>
> **2 Kings 4:13 (NIV)**

Elisha then persisted again to bless the Shunammite by inquiring if she desired a son. She replied:

> *"No, my lord!" she objected. "Please, man of God,*
> *don't mislead your servant!"*
>
> **2 Kings 4:16**

Even though she could have asked for a child—which she desired—she didn't. The Shunammite woman characterizes a woman content with her life. The Apostle Paul reminds us in Philippians 4:11-12:

> *I am not saying this because I am in need, for I*
> *have learned to be content whatever the circum-*
> *stances. I know what it is to be in need, and I*
> *know what it is to have plenty. I have learned the*
> *secret of being content in any and every situation,*
> *whether well fed or hungry, whether living in*
> *plenty or in want.*

Do we live a life of contentment where the resources and blessings of God help us realize that we are God's favored children?

## Selected Scriptures

- Isaiah 58: 6-11

- Ezekiel 16:49

- Proverbs 11:24-25

## Prayer

O Lord, help me to understand that it is more blessed to give than to receive. Amen.

## Reflection

What are the benefits of having a giving spirit?

The cycle of giving is we give, our needs are met, and as a result, we have an increase in materials. What does the cycle of giving mean to you?

## My Action

Clean out your house and give away clothes, shoes, and other items to bless others.

# DAY THIRTY-ONE
# Psalm 143

During the Lenten season, it is customary to read and pray the seven penitential psalms (6, 32, 38, 51, 102, 130, and 143). Prayerfully reciting these psalms helps us to recognize our sinfulness, express our sorrow, and ask for God's forgiveness.[58] "Though the penitential psalms were written in response to situations and transgressions that were relevant at the time for its writers, the fact remains that man's brokenness and aptitude for falling into sin have not changed over the centuries."[59]

The seven penitential psalms are composed of three similar structures:

1. A cry for help amid adversity

2. The description of the current dire circumstances

3. A specific request for help[60]

As we examine our psalm for reflection, David is in the

---

58 www.usccb.org/prayer-and-worship/liturgical-year/lent/seven-penitential-psalms-songs-of-suffering-servant.

59 www.christianity.com/wiki/christian-terms/what-are-the-penitential-psalms.html?amp=1.

60 Ibid.

midst of enemy oppression, and he desires time alone with God. However, despite the pressures that David faces and the depression that tries to cripple him, he remembers the good things that God has done in his life.

David asks God for four things in the text:

1. Save me because of your faithfulness and righteousness (Psalm 143:1)
2. Save me because I reach out to you (Psalm 143:6)
3. Save me because I hide myself in you (Psalm 143:9)
4. Save me because of your name's sake (Psalm 143:11-12)[61]

David then calls upon God's grace and mercy to overcome his enemies, recognizing himself as God's servant.

## Selected Scriptures

Psalm 77:6

Psalm 22:24

Psalm 54:5

---

61 Willmington, Harold L., The Outline Bible, (Wheaton: Tyndale House Publishers, Inc., 1999), p. 294.

## Prayer

O Lord, in my times of adversity, deliver me from my circumstances and help me to remember your goodness. Amen.

## Reflection

When was the last time you had quiet time with God? Where did you go? What did you do? Did you read, pray, or meditate? Did you sit in silence?

When was the last time God delivered you from your enemies? What happened? How did you know that it was God's deliverance?

## My Action

Before the Lenten season is over, make time for a one-day retreat. Focus your time on God. Reestablish some spiritual disciplines like reading the Bible, memorizing scriptures, and meditating on God's Word.

## DAY THIRTY-TWO
# Philippians 1:1-11

Sixth Thursday of Lent

Prayer has always been my lifeline to God. I always feel closest to God when I pray and preach. According to my mother, when I was a child, I always liked to lead the family in prayer during our Sunday dinnertime. Praying for others was a gift. I guess I was an intercessor back then, but I didn't know it! I now recognize that fervent praying for others, though difficult, is a holy privilege that brings me joy.

Prayer is the discipline that guides us into an everlasting communion with God. Prayer has power over everything! It is a powerful tool with mysterious power. How many times have you prayed, and you knew it was only God that could have answered your requests?

I believe that prayer is one of the most underutilized disciplines in our churches and personal lives. Even though prayer is hard work, our communication with God is crucial to our spiritual well-being. The Apostle Paul reminds us in Philippians 4:6, "Do not be anxious about anything, but in every situation, by prayer and petition, with thanksgiving, present your requests to God."

During COVID, I offered a once-a-month Zoom platform for women to assemble and pray, something I felt called by God to do. *"What Happens When Women Pray?"* brought countless stories of excitement and prayer/praise results.

During our prayer time, I witnessed women praying for each other, their marriages, family, children, jobs—the list was endless. I watched as women became more confident in praying and praying aloud for others. I witnessed women believe that God could and would answer their prayers.

As the text opens, Paul is writing to the pastors, deacons, and all Christians in Philippi for whom he prays. Paul reminds them in verses 3-4 that "Every time I think of you my heart was filled with joy." I resonated with the sentiments of Paul because God placed a need in my heart for women to gather and pray. To experience the laughter, the tears, the praise reports—and sometimes the technical Zoom glitches—was worth the minor headaches.

Paul explains that he prays for the Philippian believers because they assisted him when he was in and out of prison. Paul further reiterates to the Philippian church that he prays:

- God's Word is carried to its completion in the life of every believer until the return of Christ.
- That they be filled with love.
- That they might have the spirit of discernment.
- That they are filled with the fruits of righteousness.

## Selected Scriptures

- Romans 1:9-10

- Acts 2:42

- Acts 16:12-40

## Prayer

O Lord, give me the desire to intercede for others. Amen.

## Reflection

How is your life blessed and enriched by praying for others?

Intercessory prayer is one way to pray. Reflect on other methods of praying (i.e., Prayer of Thanksgiving, Prayer of Healing, and Prayer of Faith).

## My Action

For the remainder of the Lenten season, choose one person to intercede for daily.

# DAY THIRTY-THREE
# Psalm 31: 9-16

Sixth Friday of Lent

It has been disturbing in life to feel sometimes that the African American culture is still an enemy to society. African Americans have contributed greatly to this country in so many profound ways (and interestingly, invented the folding chair, gas mask, traffic signal, automatic elevator doors, potato chips, and the Super Soaker children's water toy gun).[62] However, the shooting of young black males and females by police officers is still a major issue in our country. There are times in my life and on this Christian journey when I feel the various attacks of the enemy.

However, the Bible reminds us in Matthew 5:44, "But I tell you, love your enemies and pray for those who persecute you." The Bible also reminds us that the enemy and evil never win:

> *Do not fret because of those who are evil or be envious of those who do wrong; for like the grass they will soon wither, like green plants they will soon die away. Trust in the Lord and do good.*

**Psalm 37:1-3b**

---

62 www.voanews.com/amp/everyday-things-created-by-black-inventors/6480850.html.

An enemy is "a person who feels hatred for, fosters harmful designs against, or engages in antagonistic activities against another; an adversary opponent."[63]

Psalm 31 gained a special place in Christian devotion and liturgy when Jesus, in Luke's gospel, used Psalm 31:5 as the final prayer of his life: "Into your hands I commit my spirit" (Luke 23:46).[64] Psalm 31 is an individual prayer in which David expresses confidence in God to rescue him from his enemies.

Psalm 31 is divided into three parts. The first part is a prayer (verses 1-8). It opens as David pleads with God for protection and to position himself as a refugee. He ends this section with a promise of praise and hope for deliverance. The second part, verses 9-18, opens with, "Be merciful to me, Lord, for I am in distress," and he continues to describe the trouble within himself and with others. The third part, verses 19-23, concludes with praise and thanksgiving for God's goodness and unfailing love.

---

63 https://www.dictionary.com/browse/enemy.

64 Mays, James L., Interpretation A Bible Commentary for Teaching and Preaching , Psalms, (Louisville: John Knox Press, 1994), p. 142.

## Selected Scriptures

- Psalm 18:2

- Psalm 6:7

- Psalm 17:7

## Prayer

O Lord, I have confidence and trust that you will deliver me from the hands of my enemies. Amen.

## Reflection

Do you sincerely trust that God will deliver you from your enemies? What is your evidence?

Reflect on verse 5, "Into your hands I commit my spirit; deliver me, Lord, faithful God." What does this verse mean to you?

## My Action

The Bible instructs us to pray for our enemies. Make a list of your enemies and pray for them consistently for the next three days.

## DAY THIRTY-FOUR
# Mark 10:32-34

Sixth Saturday of Lent

In today's reflection, Jesus predicts his betrayal, death, and resurrection. As they were on their way to Jerusalem, the disciples were amazed while the followers were fearful. Most certainly, Jesus' death and resurrection should not have surprised the disciples. Jesus had tried to prepare them for the inevitable:

> *"We are going up to Jerusalem," he said, "and the Son of Man will be delivered to the chief priests and the teachers of the law. They will condemn him to death and will hand him over to the Gentiles, who will mock him and spit on him, flog him and kill him. Three days later he will rise."*

**Mark 10:33-34**

I'm not sure the disciples understood what Jesus was telling them for yet the third time. Because he often spoke in parables, perhaps the disciples thought this story was another parable. However, he did assure them he would be resurrected.

For us, Jesus' resurrection symbolizes triumph from death to life, grief to glory, and victim to victorious.

Through the Resurrection, Jesus Christ establishes victory over sin, Satan, and death. As believers, we hold the same power and victory over sin, Satan, and death. As we read, let us ponder these questions:

- Do you know and understand the magnitude of the Resurrection?
- Do you realize that without Good Friday, the Resurrection would be impossible?
- Do you know that we serve a risen Savior with many eyewitnesses?
- Do you understand that with Jesus, you have the keys to eternal life?

First, to understand the magnitude of the Resurrection, one must grasp that the Resurrection is essential to the Christian faith. Paul writes in 1 Corinthians 15:12-14, "But if it is preached that Christ has been raised from the dead, how can some of you say that there is no resurrection of the dead? And if Christ has not been raised our preaching is useless and so is your faith."

Some Corinthians taught that there was no resurrection. Some believed that the resurrection had already happened—an early teaching of Gnosticism. Gnostics believed in a spiritual resurrection rather than the Christian belief in a physical-body resurrection.

Without the Resurrection, there is no need for you to act on your faith. Without the Resurrection, your faith is meaningless, and our preaching is pointless. Without the Resurrection, we could not place our hope in a glorious future. The Resurrection of Jesus Christ is central to the Christian faith. We serve a risen Savior, who bore our infirmities and was wounded for our transgressions. Death could not keep Christ in the grave.

Secondly, to understand the magnitude of the Resurrection, one must understand that our sins are forgiven. Jesus sacrificed himself to God so that all our sins could be pardoned. Too many of us take the sacrifice of Jesus for granted. We romanticize the event so much so that we forget the pain and suffering Jesus Christ endured for humanity. Romans 4:25 states, "He was delivered over to death for our sins and was raised to life for our justification." The Resurrection verifies that Christ's death dealt decisively with our sins. Jesus Christ suffered in our place.

Finally, to further understand the magnitude of the Resurrection, one must understand the power of the Resurrection. When we remember the Resurrection, we celebrate the Holy Spirit's power that raised Christ from the dead. This remembrance gives us hope and reminds us of the victory on Golgotha's Hill.

Philippians 3:10 states, "I want to know Christ—yes, to know the power of his resurrection and participation in his sufferings, becoming like him in his death." By rising from the dead to sit at the right hand of God, Jesus fulfilled God's promise for humanity as revealed in the words of John 3:16: "For God so loved the world that he gave his one and only Son, that whoever believes in him shall not perish but have eternal life." As believers, we have the power to conquer sin, fight the enemy, and witness to the lost.

## Selected Scriptures

- Matthew 27:1-2

- Acts 2:23

- Acts 3:13-15

## Prayer

O Lord, the Resurrection proves that our sins have been paid in full, and we are granted eternal life. Amen.

## Reflection

Reflect on the statement, "The Resurrection proves that Jesus Christ was who he said.

Reflect on the statement, "The Resurrection guarantees that God can raise us from the dead."

### My Action

The Resurrection of Jesus appears in all four gospels; read all four stories.

# Sixth Sunday in Lent

## My Personal Reflection Notes

*Reflect on this past week.*

What day stood out during this week's Lenten journey?

What did you learn about yourself and your relationship with Jesus Christ?

Which "My Action" of the week brought you great joy or difficulty? Why?

Please journal your thoughts. (Space is available on the next page for journaling.)

# John 12:1-11

Sixth Monday of Lent

Today's text, the story describing Mary of Bethany's anointment of Jesus shortly before his death, has always had a profound influence on my Christian journey. For me, Mary models the unconditional love and respect she had for Jesus. The unconditional love she displays is known as *agape* love. In Christianity, *agape* is the highest level of human love for God and God's love for humanity. It is always compared to *eros* (erotic) and *philia* (brotherly) love.

Mary didn't care what the disciples said or thought about her as she anointed Jesus with her hair. In fact, she completely disregarded Jewish custom by letting her hair down in public—an act that a respectable Jewish woman would never do. However, Mary was adamant in displaying her love and service to the Master.

According to the *Merriam-Webster Dictionary, love* is described as "a strong affection for another arising out of kinship or personal ties." I believe that love is the motivation for our Christian discipleship. Jesus reminds us in John 13:34-35 (CEB):

*I give you a new commandment: Love each other.*
*Just as I have loved you, so you also must love*
*each other. This is how everyone will know that*
*you are my disciples, when you love each other.*

In today's text, Mary takes a bold step to anoint Jesus' feet with a pint of pure nard, an expensive perfume, and wiped his feet with her hair. Interestingly, all the disciples joined Judas in chastising Mary for wasting a year's wages on the perfume. However, Jesus defends Mary's act of love by replying, "Leave her alone; it was intended that she should save this perfume for the day of my burial. You will always have the poor among you, but you will not always have me." Mary's act of servanthood was a sacrifice for Jesus.

What have we as believers sacrificed for our Lord and Savior? People often question me about the personal sacrifices I have endured for the sake of ministry, but I do not feel that life in ministry has been a sacrifice for my personal life. My love and service for Christ are a gift from God. God chooses whom God calls, and we choose to answer.

As I ponder this story on my Christian journey, I see Mary as a model for us as believers. I serve the Lord because, like Mary, I want to please Jesus. I want to preach, teach, and live God's Word before humanity. My motivation in serving Christ is that God loved me so much that God sacrificed *his only son* for me. Jesus took my sins on the cross to reconcile me to God. I don't know of any human beings—except my parents—that could display this type of *agape* love. Love for Christ should be the motivation in all we do. Jesus is more than worthy for me to devote my life and service to the Kingdom of God.

Mary's action of sitting at Jesus' feet (Luke 10:39) was the first indication of her humility and love for Christ. She knew that Jesus was worthy of her love as he had also raised her brother, Lazarus, from the grave. For me, Mary displays unconditional love, service, and witness for Jesus Christ.

## Selected Scriptures

- John 13:29

- Luke 10:38-42

- John 11:43-45

## Prayer

O Lord, I'm so glad you sacrificed for me. Let my love and service be a witness to humanity. Amen.

## Reflection

What is your motivation for serving Jesus Christ? Has it been costly? Are you concerned about what others think of you as you serve Christ?

Can people smell the fragrance of Jesus Christ when they encounter you? Give examples.

## My Action

Think of someone who has shown love and sacrificed for you. Show your appreciation by displaying an act of kindness in return.

# Psalm 71:1-14

Sixth Tuesday of Lent

When I was a little girl, I liked to sit at the feet of three older women: Mrs. Sarah Simmons, Willie B. Williams, and Amanda Smith. These three women were my grandmother, my piano teacher, and my Sunday school teacher at Brannen Chapel UMC in Statesboro, Georgia. They took me under their wings and gave me sage advice about the Bible and other things. I always felt special and looked forward to spending time with each of them in their homes. My mother always told me, "Sharma, you have an old soul," a statement I didn't fully understand until I was older.

As I reflect, I cherished my moments with the "mothers of Brannen Chapel." They taught me a lot. I believe there is great wisdom obtained from listening to the older generation.

According to scholars, Psalm 71 was written by an older, anonymous saint who trusted God his entire life. The psalm is divided into four parts. Verses 1-8 describe the psalm as a prayer of confidence. It begins with a statement of faith, "In you, Lord, I have taken refuge; let me never be put to shame." It is comprised of repeated petitions interwoven with statements of trust and descriptions of trouble.

In these verses, the older psalmist describes how God has been his constant source of strength and protection. He recognizes that God has been with him, guiding him since birth. He also acknowledges that God has always remained faithful throughout his years. The "mothers of Brannen Chapel" would share stories about their faithful journey with God. Mrs. Amanda Smith often said, "If you're going to trust anyone, why not trust God?" She assured me that a relationship with Jesus Christ is what everyone needs and that the Lord will fight **all** your battles!

Verses 9-13 describe the psalmist's prayer of remorse. The psalmist asks God, "Do not cast me away when I am old; do not forsake me when my strength is gone."

Next, verses 14-21 describe the psalmist's prayer of commitment. The psalmist is committed to God in the face of trouble. He relies on God because his faith is anchored in the Lord. Verse 14 states, "As for me, I will always have hope; I will praise you more and more."

Verses 22-24 describe the psalmist's prayer of celebration. The older psalmist ends the psalm by praising God with instruments and his lips.

## Selected Scriptures

- Psalm 140:4

- Psalm 7:2

- Psalm 106

- Psalm 35:28

## Prayer

O Lord, I am never too old to serve You! Let me continue to put my trust in You. Amen.

## Reflection

How do you anticipate serving God when you are in your retirement years?

The psalmist was older and saw his life as a "portent" (verse 7). What does this term "portent" mean to you?

## My Action

The next time you visit someone in a nursing home or assisted living, ask them to share their testimony.

# DAY THIRTY-SEVEN
# John 13:21-32

Sixth Wednesday of Lent

Have you ever been betrayed by a family member, friend, or significant other? The answer, of course, is probably yes! Anytime this question is asked, the betrayal of Jesus by Judas comes to my mind.

"Betrayal is the sense of being harmed by intentional actions or omissions of a trusted person.  The most common forms of betrayal are harmful disclosures of confidential information, disloyalty, infidelity, and dishonesty."[65] The word *betray* appears approximately fifty-five times in the Bible. Several Bible scriptures speak on betrayal. For instance:

- "At that time many will turn away from the faith and will betray and hate each other" (Matthew 24:10).

- "Even my close friend someone I trusted, one who shared my bread, has turned against me" (Psalm 41:9).

- But Jesus asked him, "Judas, are you betraying the Son of Man with a kiss?" (Luke 22:48).

---

65 https://pubmed.ncbi.nlm.nih.gov/20035927/.

Never doubt that our Lord and Savior understands your feelings, as he faced the betrayal of two of his disciples: Judas and Peter.

Jesus predicts Judas' betrayal three times in the Bible, and it is depicted in the four gospels during the Last Supper as well as in the Acts of the Apostles. Despite Judas' infamous notoriety, little is known about him. Some scholars even debate whether Judas is only a fictional character. The only thing we know about Judas is that he was a disciple of Jesus who betrayed him for thirty pieces of silver.

As we open the text of John 13:21-32, Jesus predicts Judas' betrayal by saying, "Very truly I tell you, one of you is going to betray me." The disciples, at a loss for words, stare at one another trying to identify which one of them he means. In John 6:70, Jesus states, "Yet one of you is a devil." In the next verse, John affirms that Jesus is talking about Judas.

The text further reveals that Judas, leaning back against Jesus, asks, "'Lord, who is it?' Jesus answered, 'It is the one to whom I will give this piece of bread when I have dipped it in the dish.' As soon as Judas took the bread, Satan entered him. So Jesus told him, 'What you are about to do, do quickly.'" After Judas betrays Jesus, the Bible records that Judas hangs himself. I believe there are spiritual consequences for those who have committed betrayal. Following the arrest of Jesus, Peter betrays Jesus three times by denying that he knows Jesus.

When you were betrayed, did the betrayal cause you to lose sleep or affect your appetite for days or weeks? Were

BISHOP SHARMA D. LEWIS

you so disappointed that you began to question your ability to judge a person's character? Why did the betrayal hurt so much? Was it because you never fathomed that a family member could commit such an act? Was it because you shared your deeply intimate thoughts, feelings, and secrets with your friend? Was it because the pain caused by the significant other brought many personal unresolved issues to the surface?

According to psychologists, there are three ways to handle betrayal. First, you must forgive the person who betrayed you. Secondly, you must work to repair the relationship. And lastly, you must avoid future problems of betrayal by setting clear boundaries.

## Selected Scriptures

- Matthew 26:20-30

- Mark 14:17-26

- Luke 22:14-30

## Prayer

O Lord, please help me to forgive the person who betrayed me. Help me to reconcile with the person I betrayed. Amen.

163

## Reflection

Why does the betrayal of a friend, co-worker, or loved one hurt so badly? What unresolved personal issues came to the surface because of this betrayal?

## My Action

If you have betrayed someone, seek forgiveness. If you have been betrayed, seek to forgive and possibly reconcile with this individual.

# John 13:1-17, 31b-35

## Maundy Thursday

I remember the first Maundy Thursday service I experienced at Ben Hill UMC in Atlanta. I was the student minister of children's ministry, and the senior pastor, Rev. McCallister Hollins, asked all the clergy staff to participate. This service was a new experience and practice for me, as my small Methodist church in Statesboro only worshiped and took communion to commemorate this day.

The Maundy Thursday service at Ben Hill UMC enhanced my biblical understanding of the terms *servant* and *servanthood*. The Bible displays many examples of servanthood. Of course, the primary theme of the Bible is the greatest servant, Jesus Christ. Scripture gives us many examples of Jesus modeling servanthood. My favorite scripture is found in Mark 10:45, "For even the Son of Man did not come to be served, but to serve, and to give his life as a ransom for many." All believers are called to servanthood ministry. Therefore, we are called to serve others for the upbuilding of the Kingdom of God.

In John 13, we witness Jesus' disciples all gathered in the Upper Room for the evening meal. Then Jesus assumes the role of the servant and begins washing each of his disciples' feet. This meal marks the last time Jesus and his disciples break bread together before he is crucified on the cross.

The practice of foot-washing was a Jewish custom that originally started as an act of hospitality for a guest. Because the men wore sandals and walked on dirty, dusty roads, their feet were normally washed by the servant of the household before they gathered for a meal.

The Maundy Thursday service at Ben Hill UMC began with our clergy staff reenacting The Last Supper in the Upper Room where the foot-washing occurred. We then moved from the sanctuary to the fellowship hall to wash the feet of the members we served at Ben Hill. At first, I wondered: how am I supposed to wash feet? How would I feel? Would the members be embarrassed to show us their feet?

I remember kneeling with a pillow to cushion my knees and a white towel to dry the feet. I can't remember the person's feet I washed first, but I remember the feeling. I felt a strong sense of honor and humility to be washing the member's feet. I remember holding back my tears as I watched people, one by one, display their gratitude, love, and appreciation by hugging our necks. As time passed, I thought, "This is what Jesus did with his disciples!"

After we finished the foot-washing of the members, my senior pastor washed all ten of the clergy staff's feet. I watched in amazement that the *senior* pastor of Ben Hill UMC washed *my* feet! After all, I was only a student minister of children's ministry. The Holy Spirit revealed to me at that moment that it wasn't about my clergy status; it was that my senior pastor was displaying love and servanthood. It was General Bruce C. Clark of the

166

U.S. Army that stated, "Rank is given you to enable you to better serve those above and below you. It is not given for you to practice your idiosyncrasies." I then watched the senior associate pastor wash the feet of the senior pastor as we gathered around and laid hands on him and prayed. This moment is forever etched in my mind and my ministry.

After Jesus washes his disciples' feet and identifies his betrayer, he provides these words for us:

> *A new command I give you: Love one another. As I have loved you, so you must love one another. By this everyone will know that you are my disciples, if you love one another.*
>
> **John 13:34-35**

Jesus washing the feet of his disciples in this intimate moment exemplifies to us as Christians that servanthood is essential to what it means to be a follower of Jesus Christ.

## Selected Scriptures

- Matthew 20:26-28

- John 8:42

- John 15:12-13

## Prayer

O Lord, teach me how to follow your examples of serving others. Amen.

## Reflection

Do you feel called to serve others? Describe your understanding of the act of servanthood. What motivates you to serve others?

Describe the last time you experienced the act of servanthood being carried out. What happened?

## My Action

Participate in a Maundy Thursday foot-washing/communion service in your community and invite a friend or family member to accompany you.

## DAY THIRTY-NINE

# Psalm 22

### Good Friday

Today, in Christendom, we commemorate Good Friday, the crucifixion of Jesus and his death on the cross. This day marks the climax of Jesus' life and allows us as Christians to reflect on his suffering and sacrificial death. Many church services are held between noon and three p.m. to commemorate the hours Jesus hung on the cross. Christians observe this day through prayer, fasting, and reading of scriptures from the gospels.

Psalm 22 is a lament psalm known as a "prayer of help." The psalm is structured into three parts:

1. A prayer for help (verses 1-11)
2. A cry for deliverance (verses 12-21)
3. A song of praise that connects David with the Messiah (verses 22-31)

Remarkably, this psalm simultaneously captures the life experiences of David and Jesus. They both felt abandoned by God, and both endured the suffering from their enemies.

On this Christian journey, have you ever felt abandoned

by God? Have you ever wondered if God even heard your prayers in the quiet of the night? No matter how hard life may be or what you experience, God has no intentions of abandoning you. John 14:18 (NLT) affirms, "No, I will not abandon you as orphans—I will come to you." As a result of their situation, they called out to God for deliverance and celebrated that God always defends the oppressed.

In the opening words of Psalm 22, David speaks of his suffering—the same words that Jesus utters from the cross—"My God, my God, why have you forsaken me?" Scholars suggest that Psalm 22 is unique because verse 1a is the fourth word quoted from the cross as Jesus bears our sins. The scripture further reveals that David and Jesus share two important things in common: they are both taught to love God, and they both call on God to deliver them from life-threatening troubles.

David loved God because God protected him when he faced Goliath and other enemies. David loved God by putting his faith into action, as he was known to be "after God's own heart." Jesus loved God because he was the Son of God, fully human and fully divine. Jesus loved God because he chose to suffer at Calvary as a sign of his love and obedience to the will of God. In the texts, David and Jesus both call on God for deliverance from their troubles. Psalm 55:22 reminds us, "Cast your cares on the Lord and he will sustain you; he will never let the righteous be shaken."

Isn't it comforting to know that God will never allow you to go through troubles alone?

*Be strong and courageous. Do not be afraid or terrified because of them, for the Lord your God goes with you; he will never leave you or forsake you."*

**Deuteronomy 31:6**

Finally, in the text, David praises the Lord for defending the oppressed and prays that all those who follow the Lord will live forever.

## Selected Scriptures

- Matthew 27:46
- Psalm 68:30
- Hebrews 2:12

## Prayer

O Lord, you suffered on the cross to reconcile me to God. Amen.

## Reflection

Do you have abandonment issues? How does abandonment affect individuals?

Have you ever felt abandoned by God? What does the Bible say about feeling abandoned?

## My Action

Attend a Good Friday service in your community. Invite a friend or family member to accompany you.

# John 19:38-42

Holy Saturday

I have always been intrigued by cemeteries. As a child,
I never feared the final resting place of men, women, and
children. I think my fascination was birthed because my
godmother, Mrs. Ruth Payton Alexis, owned Payton's
Funeral Home in Statesboro, Georgia. When I was not
working at our family business, I was down the street
hanging out with my god-sister, Theresa, at the funeral
home. As kids, we played and wandered through the
funeral home, being nosey and inquisitive. A distinct smell
of embalming fluid always permeated through the air, and
the air was notably cool in certain areas. Interestingly,
the ministry of mortuary science and the pastoral care for
families during this time of bereavement has always had a
profound effect on me.

I have always felt that the last portion of a funeral or
memorial service, known as the "interment," is the most
sacred moment for families and friends to help bring
closure to the loved one's death. I remember as a child—
and now as a clergyperson—walking through the cemetery
reading the various headstone epitaphs. As I would read, I

could picture the person because epitaphs tell a short story about the deceased. I saw words like "Devoted Father," "Beautiful Lady," "Never Stop Singing," "Step Softly," "A Dream Lies Here," and "She Was One Who Followed Dreams and Stars." I always felt a sense of peace and an air of sadness when I would walk around the cemetery.

When you are laid to rest, what will they put on your headstone epitaph? "Courageous Leader," "Prayer Warrior," "Believer" or "Lover of Life?" What would the headstone epitaph of Jesus say: "Son of God, Healer, Teacher, Redeemer?"

John 19:38-42 opens, "Joseph of Arimathea asked Pilate for the body of Jesus." Little is known about Joseph, except he was a converted Jew, a secret disciple of Jesus, and a rich member of the Jewish Council who had not agreed with their decision (Luke 23:50). "With Pilate's permission, he came and took the body away."

The text further reveals that Nicodemus, another secret disciple of Jesus and member of the Jewish Council, brought a mixture of myrrh and aloes; then together, he and Joseph prepared Jesus' body and later buried him in a rich man's tomb.

Scholars believe they buried Jesus in a new tomb:  a) because the tomb was owned by Joseph of Arimathea; b) because to be buried in a tomb not yet used was a special honor reserved only for the wealthy and the kings of Judah—which perhaps was a reference to his royalty; and c) some think John emphasized the "new tomb" so that after the Resurrection, there could be no mistake in the identity of the burial place.[66] Finally, according to Jesus' customs, Jesus' burial was on the same day as his crucifixion (Deuteronomy 21:22-23).

When you are laid to rest, what will people remember about you?

## Selected Scriptures

- Matthew 27:57-60

- Luke 23:50-56

- Isaiah 53:9

## Prayer

O Lord, when I am laid to rest, let my light so shine before men, women, and children. Amen.

---

66 https://www.trusting-in-jesus.com/burialofjesus.html.

## Reflection

Are you a secret disciple of Jesus Christ? Do you hide your faith from family, friends, and co-workers?

Reflect on your life. What would you want your headstone epitaph to say? Where would you like to be buried? Why?

## My Action

Visit a nearby cemetery. Take time to read the headstone epitaphs.

## EASTER SUNDAY
# Resurrection of the Lord

## My Personal Reflection Notes

*Reflect on this past week.*

What day stood out during this week's Lenten journey?

What did you learn about yourself and your relationship with Jesus Christ?

Which "My Action" of the week brought you great joy or difficulty? Why?


Please journal your thoughts.

Made in the USA
Columbia, SC
09 March 2023

13566457R00102